AVERY CARD

WINNING CARIBBEAN STUD POKER

and

LET IT RIDE

AVERY CARDOZA'S
WINNING
CARIBBEAN
STUD POKER
and
LET IT RIDE

Avery Cardoza

Cardoza Publishing

Visit our Web Site! www.cardozapub.com

Cardoza Publishing, Publisher of Gambling Research Institute books, is the foremost gaming and gambling publisher in the world with a library of close to 100 up-to-date and easy-to-read books and strategies. These authoritative works are written by the top experts in their filds and with more than 5,000,000 books in print, represent the best-selling and most popular gaming books anywhere.

PRINTING HISTORY

First Printing	*June 1998*
Second Printing	*March 2000*

ISBN: 0-940685-12-4
Library of Congress Catalog Card Number: 97-94717

Write for your free catalogue of gambling books, advanced and computer strategies.

CARDOZA PUBLISHING

PO Box 1500 Cooper Station, New York, NY 10276
Phone (718)743-5229 • Fax (718)743-8284
E-Mail: cardozapub@aol.com
www.cardozapub.com

ABOUT THE AUTHOR

Avery Cardoza is the foremost gambling authority in the world and best-selling author of twenty-one gambling books and advanced strategies, including *How to Win at Gambling*, *Secrets of Winning Slots*, and the classic, *Winning Casino Blackjack for the Non-Counter*.

Cardoza began his gambling career underage in Las Vegas as a professional blackjack player beating the casinos at their own game and was soon barred from one casino after another. In 1981, when even the biggest casinos refused him play, Cardoza founded Cardoza Publishing, which has sold more than five million books and published close to 100 gaming titles.

Though originally from Brooklyn, New York, where he is occasionally found, Cardoza has used his winnings to pursue a lifestyle of extensive traveling in exotic locales around the world.

In 1994, he established Cardoza Entertainment, a multimedia development and publishing house, to produce interactive gambling simulations that give players a taste of a real casino with animated and responsive dealers, and the full scale of bets at the correct odds. The result, *Avery Cardoza's Casino*, featuring 65 gambling variations, became an instant entertainment hit making its way onto USA Today's best-seller's list. It also catapulted Cardoza Entertainment, measured by average sales per title, as the number two seller of games in the entire industry for the first six months of 1997, ahead of such giants as Dreamworks, Microsoft, and others. Thier second title, *Avery Cardoza's 100 Slots*, was s simulated slots palace with 101 machines.

Cardoza Entertainment's activities in developing an online casino for real money has attracted worldwide interest in the online gambling community. As the highest profile player in casino simulations, and the only publisher featuring actual simulations with true odds and interactive animated dealers,Cardoza Entertainment is acknowledged as the leading player in the online casino market.

TABLE OF CONTENTS

SECTION III

LET IT RIDE GAMES   65

SECTION IV

SECTION V

SECTION I

OVERVIEW

I. INTRODUCTION

In this book, I'll show you everything you need to know to beat two of the hottest new table games, Caribbean Stud Poker and Let it Ride. We'll go over all the basics of play, from the actual equipment and layout, to the basic winning hands, strategies, and built-in chances of winning that you should be aware of.

There are correct ways to play Caribbean Stud Poker and Let it Ride that will improve your chances of winning, and I will present a full playing strategy for each of these games to give you the best chance possible. I will also show you advanced strategies to give you that extra edge and provide you with sane money management advice to protect you when luck is running poorly and to maximize your profits when things are going well.

In Caribbean Stud Poker, we'll look at the ranks of the hands and payout schedules, how tie hands are resolved, what the dealer's qualifying hand means and how it affects your strategies, the best times to double your bet and increase your winning chances, the ante, call bet, playing, and progressive bet strategies, the house percentage, and what the aggregate payout means to you.

In Let it Ride, we'll cover the basics of play, winning poker hands, object of the game, the player's first and second option, the third and fourth card strategies for taking down bets or letting them ride including advanced strategies, the showdown, the house percentage, the Tournament and Bonus bets, and much more to give you a complete picture on how the game is played and how you can beat the odds to be a winner.

Both of these games are similar to poker in that they share the hand values, but it is there that the similarity ends. These games are played against the casino, not against other players, there is no bluffing, and payoffs come as a result of achieving a predetermined poker hand.

Let it Ride strictly follows this formula and adds the novelty of allowing you to remove bets if you don't like your hand, which is a great feature. You can also make an additional bet which will qualify you for a large bonus payout. Caribbean Stud Poker also has the additional bet for a large payout, actually a progressive jackpot, and takes the opposite approach of Let it Ride. Here, if you like your hand, you can actually bet more after you've seen your cards. Unlike Let it Ride, where players win strictly by having hands strong enough to qualify for payouts, in Caribbean Stud Poker, the hand wins either by the dealer defaulting with a weak hand, or if the hand is strong enough, by beating the dealers hand.

There is much to learn with these new games and we'll get to that now.

SECTION II

CARIBBEAN STUD POKER

I. INTRODUCTION

Caribbean Stud Poker, which as the name suggests, caught hold and became popular in the Caribbean casinos first, has now spread and can regularly be found in Las Vegas casinos and other gambling establishments around the world.

While Caribbean Stud Poker is similar to standard poker in that both share the common rankings of the hands, it is dissimilar in most other aspects of the game. For one, Caribbean Stud Poker is played against a dealer, not the other players; for another there is none of the bluffing and skillful play inherent in regular poker.

The game is relatively simple to play. Like five card stud poker, five cards will be received by each participating player - there will be no draws. The player's only decisions are whether to call an additional bet after several cards are dealt, or whether to fold the hand and forfeit the original ante bet.

There is one other facet to the game that entices players to the Caribbean Stud Poker tables: There is a progressive jackpot that pays off as much as hundreds of thousands of dollars if a royal flush is drawn, and smaller bonus payouts for other winning hands.

Let's take a look now and see what the game is all about.

II. THE BASICS

THE SETTING

Caribbean Stud Poker is played on a table that closely resembles that of a blackjack table, with the players seated around the oval side of the table, and the dealer standing along the flat side facing the players. In front of the dealer is a chip rack holding the table's bankroll. It is from this rack that the dealer will pay off winning hands, or deposit losing bets that he has collected.

The table is usually built to accommodate seven players, with seven seats placed around the oval side, along with corresponding betting areas on the layout to mark the locations where bets can be placed. The game can be played with just one player against the dealer or with the full complement of seven players. In either case, it doesn't affect the strategy or play of Caribbean Stud Poker, for players play against the house not against each other.

The standard 52 card pack is used in Caribbean Stud Poker, with 13 cards of each rank, Ace to King, and four suits, spades, diamonds, clubs and hearts. One deck is used for play and dealt out of a shoe, a plastic oblong device used to hold the cards. The shoe is always found to the dealers left, or from the players vantage point, on their right side of the table.

Another item on the table might be the Shuffle Master shuffling machine, an increasingly popular device that automatically shuffles the cards.

In front of each player's position are three betting spots, one for each of the three bets a player can make. The first spot, closest to the player and in a circle, is marked "bet", the second spot, rectangular in shape, is marked "ante". The final betting area, closest to the dealer, is actually a drop slot, a "hole" in the table where a $1 coin or chip gets deposited to participate in the progressive jackpot.

THE OBJECT OF THE GAME

The players goal in Caribbean Stud Poker is to draw a five card poker hand that is stronger than the dealer's qualifying hand, and also, when good cards are drawn, to hold a hand that is strong enough to qualify for a bonus payout. The higher ranking the player's hand, the greater the bonus won, with the caveat that the dealer must possess a qualifying hand for the bonus to count. We'll see what this means later on.

When placing the $1 optional progressive wager in Caribbean Stud Poker, the player's goal for that bet is to draw a flush or better to receive additional bonus payouts. In particular, the player would like to get a Royal Flush, a hand that can win him hundreds of thousands of dollars.

Before we look at qualifying hands, and how that affects the game, we'll review the poker hands for players unfamiliar with their rankings.

RANKS OF THE HANDS

Following are the valid poker hands used in Caribbean Stud Poker. Hands are listed in order of strength, from the most powerful, the royal flush, to the least powerful, the hands less than A K high, which are all of equally poor value in this game.

All hands are poker hands recognized in regular high poker.

Royal Flush - An A K Q J 10, all of the same suit is called a royal flush. For example, A K Q J 10 of spades is a royal flush. The odds of being dealt a royal flush, the best hand possible in Caribbean Stud Poker, is one in 649,740.

Straight Flush - Five cards of the same suit in numerical sequence, such as the J 10 9 8 7 of clubs, is called a straight flush. This particular example is called a jack high straight flush since the jack is the highest ranking card. The ace must be used as either the highest card in the straight flush (an ace high straight flush is actually a royal flush) or the lowest card, as in A 2 3 4 5 of diamonds, to be valid. The hand of Q K A 2 3 of clubs is not a straight flush, simply a flush only.

Four of a Kind - Four cards of identical rank, such as the hand 6 6 6 6 3, is called a four of a kind. The odd card in the above example, the 3, is irrelevant and has no bearing on the rank of the hand.

Full House - A full house consists of three cards of identical rank along with two cards of an identical but different rank. 8 8 8 J J and K K K 7 7 are two examples of a full house.

Flush - Any five cards of the same suit constitutes a flush in poker. A K 7 3 2 of spades is an ace high flush in spades and Q 10 7 5 3 of hearts is a queen high flush in hearts.

Straight - Five non-suited cards in sequential order, such as 10 9 8 7 6, are a straight. When straights contain an ace, the ace must serve as either the highest card in the run, such as the ace high straight A K Q J 10, or the lowest card, as in the five high straight, 5 4 3 2 A. The cards Q K A 2 3 is not a straight. It is merely an ace high hand and will be beaten by any pair.

Three of a Kind - Three matched cards of identical value along with two odd cards (unmatched) are called a three of a kind. 7 7 7 Q 2 is an example of three of a kind.

Two Pair - Two sets of equivalently valued or "paired" cards along with an unmatched card, is a two pair hand. 4 4 3 3 A and K K 3 3 J are examples of two pair hands.

One Pair - One set of identically valued cards along with three unmatched cards are called a pair. The hand 2 2 8 4 A is referred to as "a pair of twos". Pairs are ranked in order of value from Aces, the highest, down to the deuces, the lowest. Thus, a pair of aces beats out a pair of kings, and a pair of nines wins over a pair of sixes.

Ace-King Hand - The next ranking hand in Caribbean Stud Poker is the hand lacking all above combinations but led by an Ace and a King, such as the hand A K J 5 3. This is the minimum strength hand that would be deemed a qualifying dealer hand. If both the dealer and the player hold this hand, then the highest-ranked of the remaining odd cards ranks supreme.

All Other Hands - Any hand not including any of the above combinations is a non-qualifying hand and has no value in Caribbean Stud Poker.

ODDS OF DRAWING HANDS

Following is a table showing the odds of getting dealt winning hands in Caribbean Stud Poker. These are the same odds as those in regular draw poker for the first five cards dealt.

Odds of Drawing Winning Hands	
Royal Flush	649,739 -1
Straight Flush	72,192 -1
Four of a Kind	4,165 -1
Full House	693 -1
Flush	508 -1
Straight	254 -1
Three of a Kind	46 -1
Two Pair	20 -1
One Pair	1.37 -1

RESOLVING TIED HANDS

Should both the dealer and player be dealt equivalently ranked hands, then the normal rules of poker rankings would apply to determine the more powerful hand, and therefore the winner. This typically involves using the higher ranked odd cards to determine the better hand, or in the case of flush and straight type hands, the highest cards leading those hands. We'll look at all these situation below.

Resolving Pair and AK Ties - If the player and the dealer hold the same pair or Ace King led non-pair hand, then the highest comparative odd cards would decide the winner. Should those odd cards be identical in rank, then the next highest ranking cards would be compared. If all cards are identical in value, then the hand is a push, a tie, neither side wins. For example, if the dealer has a 9 9 K J 5 and the player 9 9 K Q 4, the player wins by virtue of the Queen beating the Jack. Similarly, A K Q 7 2 beats out A K J 10 9.

Resolving Two Pair Ties - The same holds true for two pair hands. J J 7 7 K beats out 10 10 9 9 A and 8 8 4 4 10 loses to 8 8 5 5 9. When both pairs are evenly matched, the higher ranking fifth card, the odd card, determines the victor. If all cards are equally ranked, such as 5 5 3 3 2 and 5 5 3 3 2, then the hand is a tie.

Resolving Flush Ties - When the dealer and the player both hold flushes, the flush led by the highest card wins, or if that is tied, by the next highest card and so on down to the fifth card if all others are equal. In the unlikely event that both

CARDOZA PUBLISHING • AVERY CARDOZA

flushes hold identically valued cards, than the outcome is a push, neither side wins.

Resolving Straight and Straight Flush Ties
The winners of mutual straights and straight flush hands are also determined by the lead card. An Ace high straight beats any other straight, and ties against another Ace high straight. Similarly, a King high straight is stronger than a Queen high or any other lesser straight.

Resolving Three of a Kind and Full House Ties - When two players hold three of a kinds or full houses, it is the hand holding the higher ranking three of a kind that wins the pot. K K K 7 7 is a higher ranking full house than Q Q Q A A, and 9 9 9 3 4 beats out 8 8 8 Q 5.

III. THE PLAY OF THE GAME

Before any action can take place, participating players must make their initial bets. To begin the betting, each player must place at least the minimum bet in the area marked ante. The minimum and maximum bets allowable will usually be posted on a small placard in the corner of the table.

In the typical casino, $5 will be the minimum bet allowed as ante. Players may also choose to make the Progressive Bet by dropping $1 into the drop slot. For now, no money can be wagered in the area marked "bet".

Once all players are ready to go and have placed their bets in the area marked ante, the dealer is ready to get the action going. The dealer's first action is to push a button that will automatically collect the $1 progressive bets that were made. These bets will drop out of sight into the bowels of the table and a red light will go on in front of each player who made the bet to indicate that that bet was made. The ante bets will still remain as before.

The dealer is now ready to distribute the cards. Five cards will be dealt face down to each participating player. The dealer will also deal himself five cards, four face down and one face up to be viewed by all players. This face up card is known as the upcard.

Players now have a decision to make about their hand. If they feel it is good enough to beat the dealer or qualify for a bonus payout, they can call, and do so by placing an additional wager in the box marked bet. This wager must be double the ante bet. Thus, if $5 was bet as an ante, then $10 would be placed in the bet area. Similarly, if $25 was the ante, then $50 would be the additional wager placed in the bet area. In the first case, the player would have total ante and call bets of $15, and in the second case, adding $25 to $50, $75 would be the total.

To indicate that the player wishes to make this additional bet, the player places his cards face down on the table. Players that do not wish to place this additional bet must fold, and do so by returning their cards to the dealer. While their ante bet is forfeited and collected by the house, no additional money is at risk for the hand. Players that have folded no longer participate in the hand.

Each player in turn will make the decision to play on by placing the additional double bet in the "call" box, or to fold and forfeit their ante bet. This is the only playing decision players will make once the cards are dealt. Play will proceed clockwise, beginning with the player at the dealer's left (the players right side) and continuing on to the third base position, the player positioned at the dealer's far right.

Once all players have made their decisions, the dealer will turn over his remaining four down cards to reveal his final five card hand. This hand will determine whether players have won or lost on their bets. The dealer first sees if he has a qualifying hand, the minimum hand required by the rules of the game to determine if bonuses and extra payouts will occur to players with stronger hands.

THE QUALIFYING HAND

A qualifying hand is one in which the dealer has at least an Ace and a King, or a higher total such as a pair or better for his five cards. For example, A K 4 3 2 (Ace-King high), 3 3 7 9 Q (pair of threes), and 7 8 9 10 J (straight), are all qualifying dealer hands, while A Q 3 4 7 is not.

Why is a qualifying hand so important? We'll take a look at that now.

When the Dealer Does Not Have a Qualifying Hand

If the dealer does not have a qualifying hand, then all players who have remained in the game win their Ante bet, regardless of whether that hand is stronger than the player's.

For example, if the dealer holds A J 10 8 2, a non-qualifying hand, and the player holds Q 9 8 6 2 or even 7 6 4 3 2, the player wins. The dealer cannot win if his hand doesn't contain at least a hand of A K strength. Players who folded however, have already conceded defeat and lost their bets. But for players who made call bets (anyone who didn't make a call bet had to have folded), a non-qualifying dealer hand spells an automatic winning hand.

That's the good news. The bad news is that if the dealer does not have a qualifying hand, players win *only* the Ante bet. Their call bets, the ones placed in the bet area, are returned to them. They are not eligible for any Bonus payouts or even 1-1 payoffs regardless of the hand drawn. That's the tough part of the game.

Thus, if $5 was wagered on the Ante and $10 in the Bet circle, and the player happened to hold three Jacks, the total win would be only $5, the $5 paid at even money for the won ante bet. The non-qualifying dealer hand negates the 3-1 bonus that would have been paid for the three of a kind if that player's hand was stronger than the dealer's. In the above example, the $10 wager in the Bet circle would be returned.

If the dealer does have a qualifying hand, there is no automatic win. Now, the stronger hand between the dealer and the player is the deciding factor. Let's see how this works.

When the Dealer Has a Qualifying Hand
When the dealer does have that qualifying hand though, that is, at least an A K or better hand, than he'll compare his hand to each of the players to see who has the stronger hand.

As opposed to the non-qualifying situation, both the ante bet and the call bet (the wager in the "bet" area) are at stake now. The player will either win both bets or lose both, depending upon whether he has a stronger total, which would be a winner, or a weaker total, which would be a loser.

For example, if $5 were bet on the ante and $10 on the call bet, and the dealer held two jacks to the players two deuces, than the player would lose both bets for a total $15 loss since, of course, two jacks are a stronger hand than two deuces.

However, if the player has the better hand, than both bets are won instead. Each wager, the ante bet and the call bet is paid differently. Ante bets are paid at even money, 1-1, while call bets are paid according to a bonus schedule which we'll show below.

Bonus Payouts on the Call Bet	
Royal Flush	100-1
Straight Flush	50-1
Four of a Kind	20-1
Full House	7-1
Flush	5-1
Straight	4-1
Three of a Kind	3-1
Two Pair	2-1
One Pair	1-1

We'll look at an example hand to make the bonus payouts perfectly clear.

Let's say we have a $5 Ante bet, and of course, our call bet, which is double, is $10. We receive three of a kind and the dealer holds a pair of Aces. We'll win $5 for the Ante bet, plus $30 on the $10 call bet (three of a kind paid at 3-1) for a total win of $35. This would be in addition to the original $15 in bets that were made, $5 on the ante and $10 on the call. Thus, $50 would be returned to us.

34

We would not qualify for the bonus payout in the unlucky event that the dealer doesn't hold a qualifying hand. Only the ante bet would be won. We also don't qualify for bonus payouts if the dealer holds a stronger hand than our hand. In that case, not only is there no bonus payout on the call bet, but both the ante and call bets are outright losers.

Note that the dealer only wins at even money, regardless of the strength of his hand and that bonus payouts for the players are made only on the call bet itself and not on the ante.

THE MAXIMUM BONUS PAYOUT

Players must be aware that casinos have a limit on the maximum amount they'll pay winners on the Bonus Payouts. Some limits may be as low as $5,000 (even lower ones might be found), while others might go as high as $50,000 or more. This limit will be posted on the table and may read, "Bonus payouts may not exceed table's maximum payout."

How does this affect the player? Well, not in a good way if the player gets a big hand and is denied the full payout because it exceeds the maximum posted table limit. Let's look at an example. Say the player has wagered $150 on the call bet and draws a straight flush in a casino with a $5,000 Bonus Payout. Normally the player would be entitled to $7,500 (50-1 x the $150 bet). However, since the maximum bonus payout is only $5,000, the player loses out on the extra $2,500 - a big hit to take. The "penalty" would be even worse if that hand was a royal flush paying 100-1 on the bonus; now the player would only get $5,000 of the $15,000, losing out on the extra $10,000!

To protect against losing out on the full amount that should be paid on a bonus payout, players must always make sure that the maximum call bet multiplied by 100 does not exceed the bonus payout. We use the number 100 because the largest bonus, on the royal flush, pays at 100-1. If 100 multiplied by a player's call bet is greater than the casino's limit, then the drawing of a royal flush would not get the full payout. As we've just shown, it will exceed that limit.

To easily come up with the maximum bet that won't be penalized if a royal flush is drawn, divide the casino's maximum payout by 100. For example, if the maximum payout is $5,000, dividing it by 100, the player's maximum call bet should not exceed $50. And of course, if the call bet is $50, the ante, which is always half that amount, would be $25.

Or, if a player likes to think in terms of the ante, which is half of the call bet, then the maximum casino payout limit should be divided by 200 to find the largest ante bet that should be made. Using the $5,000 casino limit example above, and dividing by 200, gives us an answer of a $25 maximum ante bet that should be made, and of course, a maximum $50 call bet since that bet is always double the ante bet.

No surprise; that's the same $25 ante and $50 call bets we figured before, but came to from a different direction.

If a player likes to bet at much higher numbers, then casinos should be sought out that provide their patrons with higher maximum payouts.

IV. THE PROGRESSIVE JACKPOT

The optional wager we spoke about earlier, the Progressive bet, is made by placing $1 in the drop slot or progressive slot as it is also known, before the cards are dealt. The goal of this bet is to draw a flush or higher ranked hand to receive additional bonus payouts. While flushes, full houses, and other powerful hands would be great, what the player really would like to get is a royal flush, a hand that will win the full progressive amount.

Near each Caribbean Stud Poker table is a Jackpot Meter that goes up in value each time $1 is placed into the drop slot by any table linked up to that meter within the casino. This jackpot can be as little as $5,000 or $10,000, the general starting point after a royal flush is hit, depending upon the casino, or as high as hundreds and hundreds of thousands of dollars.

Every time prior to dealing the cards that the dealer pushes the button which collects the progressive bets, the jackpot will go up its percentage in value, and get that much sweeter. The amount each progressive bet increases the jackpot varies from casino to casino. Some casinos put in only 49¢ of each dollar played, while others, particularly larger more forward thinking casinos that understand the value of larger jackpots to draw players, may put in as much as 75¢ per dollar played to boost the jackpots faster. Obviously, the smaller the amount of money put back into the progressive, the slower the jackpot will grow.

However, the actual percentage of money that gets put back into the jackpot is not really a concern for us as players; we only care who has the highest jackpots if we're going to play for them. How they got that high is neither here nor there. How high? That is the only question we need to know. It will be no coincidence that more aggressive casinos will tend to have the highest jackpots.

As that jackpot grows, so does player interest. It's just like the lottery. The larger the jackpot, the greater the players' appetites to try and win that prize.

What does it take to win the full amount of the progressive? Why, nothing less than the big sandwich with all the dressings itself - the royal flush.

While drawing this hand would certainly be nice, a player shouldn't hold his or her breath - it's a longshot. As we saw in the earlier chart, the odds of hitting the royal flush is 1 in 649,739. But playing longshots is what much of gambling is about anyway.

There are other paying hands as well in the Progressive Jackpot. The charts on the following page show two payout schedules that a player might find. The first schedule, which might be found at a few larger casinos aggressively going after Caribbean Stud Poker players, is a liberal payout schedule that works for the benefit for the player.

The second schedule, which is more commonly found, pays much less on the four of a kind, full house, and flush hands, and that of course, is to the detriment of the player.

Liberal Payout Schedule (A)
500/250/100

Royal Flush	100% of the Jackpot
Straight Flush	10% of the Jackpot
Four of a Kind	$500
Full House	$250
Flush	$100

Common Payout Schedule (B)
100/75/50

Royal Flush	100% of the Jackpot
Straight Flush	10% of the Jackpot
Four of a Kind	$100
Full House	$75
Flush	$50

There are other payout schedules you'll find. In between the 500/250/100 liberal schedule shown above, and the 100/75/50 also shown, you may find

500/150/75, 500/100/75, 500/100/50, 500/75/50, 300/ 100/50, 250/100/50, and 150/100/50. The three numbers for each group stand respectively for the four of a kind, full house and flush payoffs. This designation is similar to video poker jacks or better machines which are known by the payoffs on the full house and flush respectively (9-6 and 8-5 machines).

These other payouts, in chart form, are shown on the following pages.

Payout Schedule C
500/150/75

Royal Flush	100% of the Jackpot
Straight Flush	10% of the Jackpot
Four of a Kind	$500
Full House	$150
Flush	$75

Payout Schedule D
500/100/75

Royal Flush	100% of the Jackpot
Straight Flush	10% of the Jackpot
Four of a Kind	$500
Full House	$100
Flush	$75

Payout Schedule E
500/100/50

Royal Flush	100% of the Jackpot
Straight Flush	10% of the Jackpot
Four of a Kind	$500
Full House	$100
Flush	$50

Payout Schedule F
500/75/50

Royal Flush	100% of the Jackpot
Straight Flush	10% of the Jackpot
Four of a Kind	$500
Full House	$75
Flush	$50

Payout Schedule G
300/100/50

Royal Flush	100% of the Jackpot
Straight Flush	10% of the Jackpot
Four of a Kind	$300
Full House	$100
Flush	$50

Payout Schedule H 250/100/50	
Royal Flush	100% of the Jackpot
Straight Flush	10% of the Jackpot
Four of a Kind	$250
Full House	$100
Flush	$50

Payout Schedule I 150/100/50	
Royal Flush	100% of the Jackpot
Straight Flush	10% of the Jackpot
Four of a Kind	$150
Full House	$100
Flush	$50

CARDOZA PUBLISHING • AVERY CARDOZA

Players should keep in mind that the progressive is a separate bet and is not affected by the results of the ante or regular call bet. For example, if the player draws a full house and the dealer miraculously (or is it disastrously?) has a four of a kind at the same time, the player would still win $250 on the $1 progressive bet (assuming the more liberal payout schedule shown) even though the call and ante bets are losers.

By the same token, the player gets the full bonus payout on the $1 progressive bet even if the dealer doesn't have a qualifying hand. Thus, players must be careful to alert the dealers to their flush or better hands when the dealer has a non-qualifying hand in case the dealer accidentally removes the cards before checking for progressive winners.

There is no maximum limit on a progressive payout as there is with the bonus payout. If the royal flush is hit, players will get paid the full amount of the progressive meter.

THE AGGREGATE PAYOFF ON PROGRESSIVES

One other casino rule comes into play on the Progressive payout. The Bonus Payout is limited to an *Aggregate* payoff on the straight flush and the royal flush. What this means is that on a straight flush hand for example, a total of 10% will

46

be paid out. Thus, if two players hold a straight flush on the same deal, they would split that 10%, in effect, getting only 5% each.

If the meter showed $12,000, the total pool of $1,200 for the straight flush would be divided evenly between the two winners at $600 each. This applies only to straight flush and royal flush hands on progressive wagers, not to the bonus payouts on the four of a kind, full house and flush hands, where each player will receive the full amount listed.

The chances of two players holding a straight or royal flush on the very same hand is so unlikely, quantum degrees more than one hundred million to 1 against (the exact odds depending upon how many other players are at the table), that this casino rule shouldn't be of great concern to you.

V. HOUSE PERCENTAGE

The odds in Caribbean Stud Poker for the ante bets are similar to American double zero roulette, which is to say, they are not kind to the player. With proper strategy, the player is trying to buck a house edge of about 5.25%, difficult odds to overcome for players trying to beat the game. If the call bets are included, the house edge drops to 2.56%. Let me explain this a bit further.

The call bets in Caribbean Stud Poker, similar to double downs in blackjack or odds bets in craps, are only placed when the player either has an even game against the house, or actually has an edge. A player never wants to increase the size of a wager or put additional money attached to a wager when there are negative expectations involved. That is counter-intuitive to a winning approach.

On average, with proper strategy, a player will make a call bet half the time, actually about 52% of the time.

To look at it another way, every second hand will involve a call bet, which is a double bet. For example, if the ante is $5, the call bet is double that, or $10. Thus, if we simulate a progression, the first bet will total one bet, the second bet will total three bets (the ante and double call bet), the third bet will be the ante bet, the fourth bet will be the three bets again, and so on.

When we add together each set of bets, we average approximately two bets per hand.

Just looking at the ante bet by itself, a player will lose at a 5.26% clip. However, when the call bets are averaged in, which when played correctly are profitable for the player, the overall house odds drop to 2.56% of the money wagered.

If we compare these odds to baccarat, craps, and blackjack, games which offer much superior odds - 1.36% in baccarat, on banker and player wages, .08% or .06% in craps if the proper bets are placed, or even an outright advantage in blackjack with correct play - and you'll understand why I'm not so hot on this table game.

At more than a 5% disadvantage on the ante bet, or 2.56% when the call bets are averaged in, players will see their bankrolls steadily bleed dry as the hours tick on and the hands get dealt. It's a relatively large house edge the way I see it, and if players try their hand long enough, they'll start to see things the way I do.

However, if players enjoy the game, and are excited by the possibilities, well, that's what gambling is all about. Gamblers could do much worse at keno, Big Six and the slots machines. As long as players realize that they're up against a big take compared to the other table games, then the game can be approached with open eyes.

On the good side, Caribbean Stud Poker is like all other gambling games; players will have their good streaks and bad streaks. With a little luck and smart money management, players can emerge with winnings in the short run.

VI. WINNING STRATEGIES

INTRODUCTION

In this section, we'll go over the playing and betting strategies that optimize a player's chances of winning at Caribbean Stud Poker. We'll discuss the ante, call and progressive bets, the best way to approach the playing decisions when it's time to call or fold, and an overall approach that gives players the best chances of walking away a winner.

We'll start with the playing strategies.

PLAYING STRATEGY

There is one crucial decision to make in Caribbean Stud Poker and that is whether to make the call wager at double the ante size, or to fold and forfeit the ante without exposing additional money to risk. In some cases, as when players have a strong hand such as three of a kind or two pairs, the strategy is fairly obvious–we want the additional money out there. On the other hand, when our cards are weak and we don't even have an A and a K, cards that will at least compete with a qualifying dealer total, the strategy is also clearcut –we'll want to fold.

The basic strategy we show below will have players playing at a near optimal level. Playing the absolute perfect optimal strategy will gain players so little as to be negligible; only a few hundredths of a percent can be gained with perfect playing strategy. It is so tiny a gain, especially when we're dealing with a negative expectation of over five percent to begin with, that the extra effort needed to learn a semi-complicated playing strategy is not worth it by any stretch of the imagination. Players need not even worry about it; the strategy presented here is all that a player needs to know.

The correct playing strategy divides hands into those which are stronger than the dealer's qualifying total of A K, which we'll generally keep, and hands which are weaker than the minimum A K, which we'll throw away and surrender the ante.

We'll look at the details below starting with the strongest hands, and work our way down to the weakest hands.

a. Two Pair or Higher. Two pair, three and four of a kind, straights, flushes, full houses, and straight and royal flushes are all very strong hands that not only are heavily favored to win, but which pay bonus payouts. The strategy for this grouping of hands is very clear even to beginning players - make the call bet!

b. Pairs. Pairs are dealt 42% of the time in five card poker, so this is a hand players will see on a regular basis. The correct strategy when holding a pair, any pair, is to call, regardless of the dealer's upcard. This is a clear gain in all situations.

Note that this doesn't mean players win money in the long run in all pair situations. For example, when holding 2's, 3's, 4's, 5's, 6's, and 7's, players long term expectations are negative, that is, they will show a loss. However, except for the lowest of pairs, the 2's-4's, players will always have a positive expectation of winning when their pair is greater than the dealer's upcard. For example, if we hold a pair of 9's, and the dealer shows an 8, we have a long term expectation of winning.

We already know that the dealer's 8 if paired and not improved with a further 8 or second pair, is a loser to our 9's.

Our strategy with these low pairs is to minimize losses, just as in blackjack when we are dealt inferior hands like 12-16 - the bust hands. In Caribbean Stud Poker, it is a mistake to throw away small pairs just because they're weak.

Yes, they may be weak, but keeping them is a lot stronger strategy than discarding them and forfeiting the ante. Players that throw away small pairs give up anywhere from 5-10% depending upon the pairs they discard. That's a bad loss to take.

Remember that the general strategy in Caribbean Stud Poker is to minimize losses in bad situations, as when we're dealt a small pair and play it for lesser losses, and to maximize winnings when our situation is strong, as when we're dealt two pair or higher. To again use a blackjack analogy, when there is a doubling down situation, which means we have the edge, we want to get more money on the table.

The strongest pairs are 10's, J's, Q's, K's, and A's. These pairs have a positive expectation of winning against all dealer upcards.

c. A K vs. Dealer. When we hold A K, we have a borderline hand whose strategy depends on the other three cards we hold, and the dealer's upcard. This is a special strategy situation based on the qualifying dealer rules of the minimum A K hand.

Following are the two breakdowns for playing A K hands.

1. When our third highest card is a J or Q, we call the dealer.

For example, the hand A K J 9 4 should be played against all dealer upcards including the A.

The thinking here is that if the dealer makes a qualifying hand of A K x x x, x standing for any other non-pairing (or cards which form a higher hand), the A K J or better hand is strong enough to win, thus making the call bet a profitable play.

2. When our third highest card is less than a J, we call the dealer only if his upcard matches one of our five up cards; otherwise we fold.

Examples: Call with A K 10 5 2 vs. A, and vs. 2, but fold A K 10 5 2 vs. Q, and A K 8 7 6 vs. 5.

The Ace-King hands are close plays that, percentage wise, are almost 50-50 for the player in terms of long term gain. To make calling a correct play, that is, a theoretical gain over not calling and folding, we need the little extra edge that favors our hand. In the situation where one of our cards matches the dealer's upcard, the dealer is that much less likely to have a pair and defeat us. There is now one less card that can help the dealer.

Therefore, under those circumstances, the correct play is to call. We use the extra piece of information (of holding a card the dealer needs) to gain that slight edge in this marginal situation.

A Q or Less vs. Dealer. Any hand that doesn't have at least an A K or better should be folded. Examples: Fold A Q J 10 9, A Q 8 7 6, K Q J 10 6, and 10 8 4 3 2.

The problem with these hands are that in essence, they're worthless. A Q led hands are no better the J high or even 8 high hands. In all cases, if the dealer qualifies, these hands are losers. Obviously, since a qualifying dealer hand, by definition, contains an A K or better, it beats all the hands in this category.

The Disadvantage of Playing A Q or Lesser Hands

There is one constant in Caribbean Stud Poker that will make the playing of A Q or less hands disastrous: The dealer will make a qualifying hand approximately 56% of the time. At first glance, you might think that the loss is $12 for every $100 bet - 56 losses less 44 wins.

That's a very convincing argument not to make this play. Giving up 12% is enormous and a foolish play. But the loss is much worse! It's equivalent to being more than ten times worse than that, about

125% when based on the ante bet! Let's take a closer look.

Here's how the math breaks down.

We'll use a $10 ante bet for this example. Of the 44 times the dealer doesn't qualify, we win a total of only $440. Since the dealer didn't qualify, only the ante bet is paid off. The $20 call bet is returned. That's $10 for each winning hand at 1-1, even money. Of the other 56 times that the dealer qualifies, we not only lose the $10 ante bet, but the $20 call bet as well! That's $1680 in losses against only $440 in wins for a net loss of $1240.

Thus for every $1,000 made in Ante bets, a loss of $1240 is 124%, actually closer to 125% (we rounded down the 56% number to show the math easier). That's a pretty heavy loss to try and beat in this game.

Making these kind of plays will destroy a player at the table. Players should never, ever think about playing these type of hands. These horrible plays are worse than any other play that can be found in the entire casino and that's pretty bad. To be a winner at Caribbean Stud Poker, you absolutely must avoid any situation that give the house an exorbitant edge.

PROGRESSIVE $1 BET STRATEGY

Generally speaking, unless the progressive jackpot is in the hundreds of thousands, the progressive $1 wager is a complete sucker bet giving the house an edge that hovers around 50% in most cases and goes as high as almost 75% in the worse case. Ouch!

Even when the jackpot is say $250,000, the player still may be giving the casino an enormous edge by making this bet. The exact edge the casino enjoys is a function of several factors - the actual bonus paid on four of a kinds, full houses and flushes, which as we've seen, varies from casino to casino; the size of the jackpot itself; and equally important, the size of the ante bet.

This last factor, the size of the ante bet, is important because the progressive bet cannot be made as an independent wager by itself. At a minimum, to play Caribbean Stud Poker, the player must place an ante bet, and then optionally, if desired, he or she can make the progressive bet as well. Since each bet gives the casino roughly a 5.25% edge, the larger the average bet, the higher the jackpot must be to compensate for these bets.

Thus, if $5 were wagered on the ante, a break-even for the progressive would be far lower than if $10 were the average ante bet.

For example, if we're playing in a casino with more liberal payouts, paying 500 for four of a kind, 250 for a full house, and 100 for a flush, and have an average $5 ante bet, then the break-even on a progressive jackpot would be around $200,000. However, if we had the less liberal payout of 100 for four of a kind, 75 for a full house, and 50 for a flush, the payout schedule found at many casinos, the break-even progressive jackpot is closer to $350,000 on that average $5 bet.

But make that $5 average ante $10, and the break-even jackpot on the more liberal rules jumps almost $100,000!

A $1 average ante bet would afford overall better odds when making the $1 progressive and hoping to land a big jackpot, but that will rarely be found. Most casinos have a $5 minimum ante bet.

Thus, as we see, these three important factors - average ante size, jackpot size, and bonus payout schedule - all influence the actual disadvantage a player faces at Caribbean Stud Poker.

Or, in the rare cases where we do find a monster payout that has built up, the progressive bet may actually be advantageous.

It's always nice to dream of the big hit, hence the millions and millions of players who play the lottery consistently, and the many players who donate the $1 to the progressive pool in Caribbean Stud Poker. However, the way I approach gambling, I would rather stick to the bets that offer me the best chances of winning in the long run. And unless the progressive jackpot is in the hundreds of thousands of dollars, we would be better off avoiding the progressive bet altogether.

If a player feels the pressing need to make that $1 "dream" bet, he might consider the lottery. Lousy odds, but if the player does hit, the payout is not a few measly tens of thousands of dollars, it's a two year cruise around the world, a dream home, instant retirement, and the most expensive cigars money can buy.

But then again, my advice is always to play with grounded rationale. Make the best bets the games can give you, and if winning, make sure to walk away with the casino money in your pocket.

BETTING STRATEGY

In Caribbean Stud Poker, there is no particular betting strategy to pursue in terms of gaining an advantage as there is in blackjack, except to bet intelligently according to one's bankroll.

A bettor should never risk money that he cannot afford to lose. That is the first rule for any betting proposition and really one of the most important rules in gambling, if not the most important rule. (We'll talk more about the concepts of bet size, betting limits, and the amount one should put at risk in the money management section.)

Occasionally, the progressive jackpot may get into the hundreds of thousands of dollars, and the bettor will be looking at a positive expectation on the progressive $1 wager. This is rarely seen, but in these instances, when we're chasing a very large progressive jackpot, a situation which actually gives us the edge, our strategy will be to keep the ante bet as small as possible to minimize the effect of the house edge on the ante and call bets.

OVERALL WINNING STRATEGY

The main thing to keep in mind with Caribbean Stud Poker is that the game is a negative expectation gamble. The casino has an advantage of 5.25% on the regular ante bets, 2,56% when the call bets are taken into account.

Theoretically, the longer a bettor plays, the closer to the 5.25% and 2.56% "taxes" that will be extracted by the inevitable house edge built-in to the game. On the progressive bet, as we discussed earlier, the house edge can soar to almost 75%, or in exceptionable cases, where the progressive jackpot is in the hundreds of thousands of dollars, can actually favor the player. But as we all know, there are up and down swings in gambling. Anyone, with a little luck, can walk away from the table a winner. But to maximize one's chances of winning, bettors must play their cards correctly and make only the best bets available to them.

A player's first order of business is to avoid the progressive bet. Unless the jackpot is enormous, at least $200,000 or more, depending upon the circumstances, this bet gives too much away to the casino. Avoiding this wager will avoid a constant drain on a player's bankroll.

Secondly, bettors must study the playing strategy so that the correct moves are made and the chances of winning are optimized. As we saw earlier, there is a lot of information to remember, but one must learn the strategies and use them all the time, not just when the mood strikes.

There is no substitute for correct play. Hunches only build the casinos bigger and make the players poorer.

Finally, intelligent money management decisions must be employed at the tables. When things are going poorly, which they sometimes do, we must limit our losses. We will never take a bad beating in any one session. And when we're on a hot streak, we'll make sure that we leave a winner.

We'll never give the casino back all our winnings once we've got a big winning streak going. That's not only the key in Caribbean Stud Poker, but in all gambling pursuits.

SECTION III

LET IT RIDE GAMES

I. INTRODUCTION

Let it Ride was first introduced to the Las Vegas casinos in August, 1993, and immediately became a rousing success. The game has continued to grow in popularity and can now be found in hundreds of casinos across the country as well as in international casinos as well. The Shuffle Master company, developer of Let it Ride, Let it Ride: The Tournament, and Let it Ride Bonus, has really hit paydirt with this game.

Why the big fuss? Well, for one, Let it Ride offers players thousands of dollars in prizes if the optional $1 bonus bet is made and a big hand is drawn. Gamblers are always attracted to jackpots.

Second, Let it Ride, like Caribbean Stud Poker, draws some of it's popularity from its similarities with poker, a game familiar to gamblers. Thus, players find Let it Ride easy to learn and play.

And third, the unique aspect of the game that lets players remove two of their three bets when they're unhappy with the cards they're dealt, is an attractive feature that strikes a responsive chord among players.

Let it Ride is a simplified version of five card poker. Players get dealt three cards, and use these in combination with the two community cards shared by all players to form a final five card hand that either qualifies for a payout, which is a winner, or is of lesser value, which is a loser.

There are no draws of additional cards, bluffing of opponents, or strategy decisions other than deciding whether to take down two of the three mandatory starting bets in the game, or whether to let them ride. Unlike other table games offered by the casino, players do not compete against a dealer or other players, winning hands are solely judged according to the strength of the five card total as it relates to the paytable.

That said, let's take a closer look at Let it Ride and see how the game works.

II. THE BASICS

THE EQUIPMENT OF PLAY

Let it Ride is played on a blackjack-style table with a single standard pack of 52 cards. On the flat side of the table is the dealer who performs all the functions one would expect; the dealing of the cards, the paying off and collection of won and lost bets, and the overall running of the game. In front of the dealer will be the chip rack, where the bankroll of the table sits in long colorful rows in full view of the players.

Across from the dealer, along the oval edge and facing him, are as many as seven participating players, trying their hand with lady luck.

On the layout itself, where the game is played and all bets are made, are three betting circles in front of each player's seat. These circles are laid out next to each other, horizontally, in front of each player's position. Going left to right, they are marked 1, 2 and $ respectively. These are the spots where the three mandatory bets are placed by each participating player.

There is one additional bet spot as well, a red button located in front of each player, where an optional $1 wager can be made on Let it Ride, The Tournament, or the new bet which has replaced the Tournament bet almost everywhere, the Let it Ride Bonus Bet.

Another item on the table might be the Shuffle Master shuffling machine, an increasingly popular device that automatically shuffles the cards.

THE OBJECT OF THE GAME

The player's goal in Let it Ride is to draw a hand that is strong enough to qualify for one of the winners in the payout schedule. These payoffs range in value from even money wins, 1-1 on a tens or better pair, to 1000-1 when the Royal Flush is hit.

When placing the $1 optional wager on Let it Ride, The Tournament, a player's additional goal is to get a straight flush or a royal flush, hands that not only pay $2,000 or $20,000 respectively, but enter that player in the big tournament which has a grand prize of one million dollars when this $1 bet is made. In the Let it Ride Bonus game the lure is a payoff as high as $10,000 or $25,000, depending upon the venue.

There is no competition against other players as in regular poker, or against the dealer as in Caribbean Stud Poker. In Let it Ride, the goal is solely to draw a hand strong enough to qualify for a payout.

HANDS THAT QUALIFY FOR PAYOUTS

As we mentioned above, the player's goal is to draw a hand that qualifies for a winning payout. The higher the rank of the hand, the greater the payout. At a minimum, a player must have a tens or better payout to be a winner. Any lesser hand fails to qualify for a payout, and the player's bets will be lost.

The best hand, the royal flush pays 1,000 to 1 in most of the casinos that offer the game. There are jurisdictions where the gaming commission has mandated that the highest payoff, that of the royal flush, be at the smaller 500-1, or where casinos have chosen this paytable for their customer.

The following charts show the winning hands and payoffs for the two basic paytables that will be found.

TYPICAL PAYOFF SCHEDULE

The following paytable is the standard one found in casinos, and features a 1000-1 payoff on a royal flush. The players get compensated more for big wins on this schedule, and less for the full house and flush wins, as we'll see.

Typical Payoff Schedule	
Royal Flush	1,000-1
Straight Flush	200-1
Four of a Kind	50-1
Full House	11-1
Flush	8-1
Straight	5-1
Three of a Kind	3-1
Two Pair	2-1
Pair of 10's or Better	1-1

ALTERNATE PAYOFF SCHEDULE

This is the other basic payoff schedule that is found in some locations. While the player receives a smaller payoff on the less frequent winners, the flush, straight flush, royal flush, and four of a kind hands, you'll see that the payoffs for the more frequently hit full house and flush hands are greater.

Either payoff chart, however, will give the player equivalent odds.

Alternate Payoff Schedule	
Royal Flush	500-1
Straight Flush	100-1
Four of a Kind	25-1
Full House	15-1
Flush	10-1
Straight	5-1
Three of a Kind	3-1
Two Pair	2-1
Pair of 10's or Better	1-1

THE WINNING POKER HANDS

For players unfamiliar with poker, or who want to brush up on their knowledge of poker combinations, we've listed the categories of valid poker hands recognized in Let it Ride. Hands are listed in order of strength, from the most powerful, the royal flush, to the least powerful, the hands which don't qualify for a payout at all.

Royal Flush - An A, K, Q, J and 10, all of the same suit is a royal flush. For example, A, K, Q, J 10, of spades, is a royal flush.

Straight Flush - Five cards of the same suit in numerical sequence, such as the J 10 9 8 7 of clubs, is called a straight flush. The ace must be used as either the highest card in the straight flush (an ace high one being a royal flush) or the lowest card, as in A 2 3 4 5 of diamonds, to be valid. The hand of Q K A 2 3 of clubs is not a straight flush, simply a flush only.

Four of a Kind - Four cards of identical rank, such as the hand 6 6 6 6 3, is called a four of a kind. The odd card in the above example, the 3, is irrelevant and has no bearing on the rank of the hand.

Full House - A full house consists of three cards of identical rank along with two cards of an identical but different rank. 8 8 8 J J and K K K 7 7 are two examples of a full house.

Flush - Any five cards of the same suit constitutes a flush in poker. A K 7 3 2 of spades is called an ace high flush in spades and Q 10 7 5 3 of hearts is a queen high flush in hearts.

Straight - Five non-suited cards in sequential order, such as 10 9 8 7 6, are called a straight. When straights contain an ace, the ace must serve as either the highest card in the run, such as the ace high straight A K Q J 10, or the lowest card, as in the five high straight, 5 4 3 2 A. The cards Q K A 2 3 of mixed suits is not a straight. It is merely an ace high hand.

Three of a Kind - Three matched cards of identical value along with two odd cards (unmatched) are called a three of a kind. 7 7 7 Q 2 is an example of three of a kind.

Two Pair - Two sets of equivalently valued or "paired" cards along with an unmatched card, are called two pairs. 4 4 3 3 A and K K 3 3 J are examples of two pair hands.

Tens or Better - One set of identically valued cards along with three unmatched cards are called a pair. The hand J J 7 4 2 is a pair of jacks. In Let it Ride, the minimum hand that qualifies for a payout is a pair of tens or higher. Thus, tens, jacks, queens, kings, and aces, are all winning totals with the 1-1 payout. Pairs of nines and lesser strength pairs don't qualify for payouts.

All Other Hands - Any hand not including any of the above combinations is a losing hand with no payouts, and thus, has no value in the regular Let it Ride table game.

III. THE PLAY OF THE GAME

Before any cards are dealt, participating players at the table must make a bet on each of the three betting circles in front of them. These bets must be made in equal amounts. For example, if $5 were to be bet on the circle marked "1", then that same $5 must be bet on the other two circles, the one marked "2", and the one marked "$".

Additionally, a $1 wager may be made on the Tournament or Bonus spot. We'll go over this bet in a little bit.

There is normally a minimum $5 bet on each circle, though smaller casinos may offer minimums as low as $3. In the first case, a minimum of $15 total would have to be bet among three bet circles, $5 per spot, and in the second case, a minimum of $9, $3 per spot, would be required.

Once all players have completed betting, and the cards are shuffled and ready to go, the dealer will deal three down cards to each player. The dealer will also deal two face down cards and place them in the two rectangular boxes imprinted on the layout in front of his position. These cards are called community cards, and will be shared by all active players to form their final five card holding.

The rules of the game disallow players from showing their cards to their fellow players at the table. The casinos don't want players to gain any untoward advantage that may help them make better playing decisions. (This is unlike regular poker where sharing card information actually hurt's a player's chance of winning since he plays against the other players at the table.)

At Let it Ride, players strategize only their own hand's winning chances. The relative strengths of other players hands has no bearing on a player's own chances of winning, though the cards those hands contain may help provide information to a player's own playing decision.

Beginning with the player on the dealer's left and proceeding in a clockwise direction, each player in turn has the following options:

THE PLAYER'S FIRST OPTION

Each player in turn, after looking at his or her three down cards, has the option of playing for the bet in circle "1", that is, letting it ride, or withdrawing that bet from play and having it returned to his or her bankroll.

Letting a bet ride is done by placing the cards under or in front of the cards in the circle marked "1". The dealer will understand this motion to mean that the player wishes to keep his or her bet in play, and will move on to the next player.

A player that wishes to remove his or her bet from play, does so by simply scraping the table with the cards. This motion will prompt the dealer to remove that player's bet from the first circle and return it to the player. Thus, any player who is unhappy with the cards dealt to him, is able to remove his or her bet from the circle marked "1".

Players should not physically take back their own bets; they should let the dealer perform that function.

Once all players have made their decision, going clockwise from the dealer's left all the way around the table to the "third base" position, the seat at the dealer's extreme right, play will move on to the next round.

THE PLAYER'S SECOND OPTION

After all player's have made their decisions on bet circle "1", the dealer now turns over one of the two community cards in front of him so that each player knows four of the five cards that will be used to form his or her final hand.

Again, just like in the first round, players are faced with the decision to let their bet in circle "2" ride, or to take it down and put it back into their bankroll. The motions are the same. Players wishing to let their wager ride slide their cards under their bet in circle "2". And those wishing to remove their bets, scrape the table with their cards. Players that elect to remove their bet in circle "2" from play will have it returned to them by the dealer.

All players may remove their second bet, the one in circle "2", even players that chose to let the bet in circle "1" ride. Each bet is independent of the previous bet. For example, one player may remove the bet in circle 1 and let the bet in circle 2 ride; another may Let it Ride in circle 1 but remove it in circle 2; a third may remove bets in both circles; and a fourth may let both bets ride. All these combinations are permissible.

When all players have completed their playing decisions on their bets in circle "2", it is time for the showdown.

LET IT RIDE GAMES

THE SHOWDOWN

The dealer will now turn over the second and last community card. By combining the two community cards with the player's three individual cards, each player will know his or her final five card hand. All cards are now exposed and each player can see how they fared on this deal.

Unlike the previous two rounds, the bet in circle "3" cannot be removed. This bet is for keeps and will now be settled by the dealer along with any other bets that the players have in the other betting circles, if any.

Going from his right and proceeding to his left, the dealer will turn over each player's cards and settle the wagers.

SETTLING THE BETS

Players who hold at least a pair of 10's or higher ranked poker hand qualify for payouts according to the payout schedule we showed earlier.

Winning hands pay out on all spots which still contain bets. For example, a player holding a pair of Jacks, which pays 1-1, and having $5 bet on each of the three spots, would win $15 total, $5 for each of the spots. Thus $30 would get returned to the player, $15 in winnings plus the original $15 wagered. If only spots 2 and 3 contained $5 bets, then

$20 would be returned to the player, $10 in which would be winnings ($5 each on circles 2 and 3).

By the same token, players whose hands didn't qualify for the payoff will lose on all spots where they had bets. At the very least, that would be one losing spot, the third circle whose bet cannot be removed, and at a maximum, three spots if the player let all bets ride. Thus, if a player bet $5, and let all bets ride, but lost, then $15 would be lost, $5 on each circle. However, if the player had removed the bets from circles 1 and 2, then only $5 would be lost.

Let's now see how the other wagers work, the $1 Progressive bet, which is being phased out, and the new Bonus Bet.

IV. THE $1 BONUS OR TOURNAMENT BET

Players have the option to make a separate $1 bet which will go toward an additional payout pool. There will be a Tournament or Bonus spot on the table to accommodate this wager, and it is made before the cards are dealt by placing $1 in the circle marked for this wager.

Formerly, this $1 bet allowed players to earn entry into the big money Let it Ride Tournament if the player drew a straight flush or royal flush hand. Beginning October 1, 1997, the tournament began to be phased out, and was replaced by a new version called the Let it Ride Bonus.

The new Let it Ride Bonus $1 side bet was introduced in October 1, 1997, to replace the $1 Tournament side wager in the Let it Ride table games.

Almost all games now feature the Bonus Bet, however, there still are a few casinos still running the Tournament.

We'll look at both of these individually, beginning with the Let it Ride Bonus wager.

LET IT RIDE BONUS

The Bonus wager works similar to the previous Tournament – a $1 bet is placed in the betting circle before the cards are drawn and winners are determined according to the hand that is drawn.

Where the two games differ is that the Bonus payout is fixed according to a set schedule and is paid out on the spot: there are no tournament playoffs as before, and no million dollar bounty waiting for the one lucky winner who goes all the way and wins the tournament.

However, this new Bonus paytable is actually much better for the average player. Rather than building a large pool of money that gets distributed to the few, the million dollar payouts are now circulated back into the regular paytables and get distributed among many. This concept is simlar to progressive slot machines. The super jackpot machines pay less out to the regular players as money is saved for the jackpot winner, while the smaller progressives keep the money flowing.

As of the time of this writing, there were twenty-four bonus paytables in effect for winners of the Let it Ride Bonus. The paytables used in a particular jurisdiction are determined by the local gaming commissions. Some areas allow just one paytable, while others approve multiple paytables that may be used. In the latter case, it is up to the casino management as to which paytable they will offer their patrons.

There is a wide range of pay schedules among these machines. Payouts for the best hand, the royal flush, range from $25,000 to $10,000; full houses can range anywhere from $75 to $200, and right on down to all the other winning hands.

Another differences occurs in the paytables as well. While some paytables give bonuses for hands as weak as a high pair (10's or better), others start paying out for two pair hands. Other games require a minimum strength of three of a kind.

The amounts that a casino pays on these wagers directly affect a players overall return on the money gambled, and of course, the house edge on the bet. With the most liberal payouts allowed, the player will buck a 3.05% house edge on the Bonus bet. The least liberal, can give the casino an edge as high as 35% or more, depending on the other payouts, steep odds for a casino bet.

Keep in mind that it is not necessarily how easy it is to get a payout on a hand that determines your overall chances of winning, but the amounts that will get paid on all winning hands overall. For example, just because one paytable makes 10's or better hands a winning combination, does not mean it has overall better odds than a paytable that pays with a minimum hand of a three of a kind.

The first three schedules, A, B, and C, show the most common payouts found.

LET IT RIDE $1 BONUS PAYOUT
Schedule A

Royal Flush	$20,000
Straight Flush	$2,000
Four of a Kind	$200
Full House	$75
Flush	$50
Straight	$25
Three of a Kind	$5
Two Pairs	$4
10's or Better	$1

Following is the second of the common Let it Ride Bonus paytables in use.

LET IT RIDE $1 BONUS PAYOUT Schedule B	
Royal Flush	$20,000
Straight Flush	$2,000
Four of a Kind	$100
Full House	$75
Flush	$50
Straight	$25
Three of a Kind	$9
Two Pairs	$6
10's or Better	No Payout

Following is the third of the common Let it Ride Bonus paytables in use.

LET IT RIDE $1 BONUS PAYOUT
Schedule C

Royal Flush	$20,000
Straight Flush	$2,000
Four of a Kind	$400
Full House	$200
Flush	$50
Straight	$25
Three of a Kind	$5
Two Pairs	No Payout
10's or Better	No Payout

As we see, each of the common paytables we've shown follow a different philosophy. Schedule A, for example, stresses frequent winners, Schedule C emphasizes less frequent winners (two pair and tens or better do not pay) with larger payouts on the three of a kind, full house, and four of a kind hands, while Schedule B mixes the two philosophies in a different blend.

Schedule D below, features the higher frequency of pay philosophy.

LET IT RIDE $1 BONUS PAYOUT
Schedule D

Royal Flush	$20,000
Straight Flush	$2,000
Four of a Kind	$150
Full House	$75
Flush	$50
Straight	$25
Three of a Kind	$4
Two Pairs	$3
10's or Better	$2

Schedule E below, shows the paytable for the game offering $25,000 for the royal flush. No surprise, the extra payoff on top means the payoffs on the bottom have to sacrifice. On this schedule, two pair and tens or better have no payoff.

LET IT RIDE $1 BONUS PAYOUT
Schedule E

Royal Flush	$25,000
Straight Flush	$2,500
Four of a Kind	$400
Full House	$200
Flush	$50
Straight	$25
Three of a Kind	$5
Two Pairs	No Payout
10's or Better	No Payout

LET IT RIDE GAMES

Schedule F below pays a healthy $10 and $6 on the three of a kind and two pair respectively.

LET IT RIDE $1 BONUS PAYOUT
Schedule F

Royal Flush	$10,000
Straight Flush	$2,000
Four of a Kind	$200
Full House	$100
Flush	$50
Straight	$25
Three of a Kind	$10
Two Pairs	$6
10's or Better	No Payout

Schedule G here is similar to Schedule F on the previous page, but with a much poorer payout on a hand by hand basis. Obviously, if there was a choice, we would play Schedule F any day over Schedule G below.

LET IT RIDE $1 BONUS PAYOUT
Schedule G

Royal Flush	$10,000
Straight Flush	$2,000
Four of a Kind	$100
Full House	$75
Flush	$50
Straight	$25
Three of a Kind	$9
Two Pairs	$6
10's or Better	No Payout

LET IT RIDE TOURNAMENT BET

Let it Ride's initial marketing push and game rules featured the $1 side bet being applied to the Let it Ride Tournament, an exciting concept which saw eligible straight flush and royal flush winners being invited to a special playoff tournament with big prizes for the winners. The rules originally allowed only 50 players to qualify for the tournament, which meant players had to have at least a straight flush of 8 or better, and as the tournament grew in popularity, it was expanded to 100 players, and then more. In 1997, four million dollars was handed out in cash for tournament winners.

However, the tournament is almost completely phased out, replaced by the Bonus game we discussed earlier. We will discuss the tournament here in case it is brought back or the player finds a rare game still offering the tournament. We suspect however, that by the end of 1998, the tournament games will become a thing of the past, unless the Shuffle Master company decides to reinstate the tournament at a later date.

While the million dollar jackpot possibilities of the $1 Tournament are the big draw of this bet, there is an additional attraction to this wager - the $1 tournament bet also qualifies the player for cash bonuses if a straight or better hand is drawn. The following chart shows these bonus payouts.

Let it Ride
$1 Tournament Payout - Bonus Payouts

Royal Flush	$20,000
Straight Flush	$2,000
Four of a Kind	$200
Full House	$75
Flush	$50
Straight	$20

The tournament bet is made by placing $1 on the red button located in front of the three betting spots. Note that while a pair of tens or higher pair, two pair, and three of a kind hands will win on the regular betting circles, they don't qualify for the bonus payouts on the $1 bet. The minimum bonus payout for this bet, as we see on the chart, is a straight or better.

We'll go over a sample bonus win for both the three betting circles and the $1 Tournament bet to make the payoffs in Let it Ride perfectly clear. Let's say the player had $5 bet, let the bets ride in all three betting spots, and drew a flush for his five cards. Each of the three betting circles would receive an 8-1 payoff (for the flush) on the $5 bet, for a $40 win per circle, or $120 total on those bets. Of course, if only one bet circle contained a bet, that win would be only $40. In addition to this win, the player earns $50 for the bonus payout on the $1 tournament bet. Thus, the total win for that round would be $120 plus $50, for a grand total of $170.

If that hand was instead a straight flush, the picture would be a whole lot sweeter. Each spot now would win $1,000 (the $5 bet at 200-1) for a total of $3,000 on the three spots, plus the bonus win of $2,000 for a grand total win of $5,000. And the really good news is that the player would automatically get entered into Let it Ride, The Tournament, where $1,000,000 could be won!

However, to receive the bonus payouts and possible entry into the tournament, the player must have made that $1 tournament wager.

LET IT RIDE - THE TOURNAMENT
The Let it Ride Tournament allows participating players the chance to win a million dollar jackpot or higher. The tournament was set up so that there were four qualifying rounds a year, each one lasting for a period of three months. These exciting and lucrative events are only open to players who

paid the $1 "entry fee" and were lucky enough to hit a straight or royal flush on that hand.

All players who receive a straight flush or royal flush during the three month qualifying period (and who had the $1 bet on the red button for the tournament bet) will be asked to fill out a tournament registration form at the time of winning. When the three month qualifying period is up, these players will be invited by the Shuffle Master Corporation to participate in the Tournament Playoffs.

And here is where the really big money can be won. At the very minimum, participants get guaranteed cash prizes beginning at $1,000. And for the lucky player who goes all the way, the grand prize of one million dollars will be the reward.

There are four rounds in the playoffs. Each player in this first qualifying round, as in every succeeding round, is given an equal amount of chips to start. Players are pitted against each other with the goal of trying to win more chips than their opponents so they can move on to the following rounds. These chips have no cash value and are only used for the purpose of determining winners on a round by round basis.

The first round gives each player a guaranteed $1,000 bonus just for playing. The top 100 winners in this first round will move on to the second round and receive an additional $1,000 bonus for their efforts, while the losers will have to settle for their original $1,000 and their "what ifs."

In this second round, players start fresh again with an equal amount of non-redeemable chips. No winnings are carried over from round one. Again, players make their best efforts to build up the winnings, hoping to be among the top winners so they can move on once again, one step closer to the million dollar grand prize.

Only the top 25 players from round two move on to round three, accompanied by another $1,000 bonus. These 25 players have now earned $3,000 in prizes, but their sights are set on going one more round, to round four where the big money prizes await. Again, chips are divided up with an equal number going to the 25 competitors.

When the dust settles, it will be only the top six players who move on to the fourth and final round and the big prizes. These six players now play for the banana split with all the fixings - three scoops, two toppings, whip cream, sprinkles, and a cherry.

In this final round, players are playing for a one million dollar prize! While the losers may be disappointed in not coming in first, they don't do too shabby either - there are $450,000 in prizes for the runners-up.

The prize schedule for the top six finalists is shown below.

Finish	Tournament Prize
1st	$1,000,000
2nd	$200,000
3rd	$100,000
4th	$75,000
5th	$50,000
6th	$25,000

V. QUICK SUMMARY OF PLAY

In this chapter, we'll briefly review the rules of play before we turn our attention to the next chapter, The Winning Strategies.

Players have a choice of removing or letting their bets ride on the first betting circle after seeing their three cards, and then on the second betting circle after the dealer exposes the first community card. All player decisions are now finished - the bet on the third betting circle cannot be removed - and the dealer will turn over each player's cards to see who won.

The player's final hand, composed of his or her three down cards and the two community cards, must be at least a pair of 10's or higher to qualify for a payoff. Hands of lesser rank than a pair of tens are losers, and the dealer will remove the lost bets. Winning hands will be paid on each circle where there is a bet.

Players who made the $1 tournament payout bet and drew a straight or better, will get paid their winnings according to the bonus payout schedule. And if the hand is a straight flush or royal flush, that player earns entry into the big tournament. On the $1 bet for the Bonus game, the same general principle applies: winning hands will be paid according to the casino's schedule.

VI. THE WINNING STRATEGIES

In this section, we'll go over the third and fourth card playing strategies for Let it Ride, the house percentages inherent to the game, and the overall strategy for winning at Let it Ride.

The main strategy considerations in Let it Ride center around the bets that have been made in the first two betting circles, 1 and 2, where the player has a choice of letting these bets ride or bringing them down and playing only for the mandatory bet in the third circle. Thus, there are two decisions to make, one for each circle.

The first decision occurs when we've looked at our three cards and decide on letting the bet ride in circle 1 or bringing it down. We'll call this the Three Card Betting Strategy. The second decision occurs when the dealer has exposed a community card, the player's fourth known card, and we must now decide the fate of the bet in circle 2. Since this occurs when we have knowledge of four of our cards, we'll call this the Fourth Card Playing Strategy.

We'll start our strategy discussions with the third card playing strategy.

THIRD CARD BETTING STRATEGY

Our first three cards give us a good indication of where the hand may be headed. We already know three fifths of the cards that will comprise our final hand and can make a clear determination on the best way to play the bets.

Sometimes, as in the case of three of a kind or a pair of tens or better, the strategy decision is obvious - we're already sitting with winners and should let the bet ride. A payout is already guaranteed and with a little luck, that hand may improve to a stronger rank and larger payoff. We'll also play strong hands that don't yet have a guaranteed payoff but which give us a positive expectation of winning.

On the other side of the coin, weak hands with negative expectations of winning will dictate a strategy of minimizing losses and the correct play will be to take down the bet in circle 1.

Below are the seven categories of Let it Ride poker hands where the optimal play is to let the bet ride in circle 1. Hands are listed from the strongest to the weakest. The reader is reminded that 10's, J's, Q's, K's, and A's, are considered high cards, cards that if paired will payoff as a winner.

Hands that We Will Play

We'll let our bet ride with the following three card hands:

1. Three of a Kind

This is fairly obvious. We've got an automatic winner guaranteeing us at least a 3-1 payoff on all our bet spots.

2. Pair of 10's or Higher Pair

Another obvious play. We already have a 1-1 payoff, and can't lose. Improving the hand will give us an even larger payout.

3. Three to a Royal Flush

We have all sorts of shots here for a payoff; a flush, a straight, a high pair (and even three of a kind and two pair), and of course, the hand we would really like to get, a Royal Flush.

4. Three to a Straight Flush

Ditto above. There are good possibilities for improvement. We should let the bet ride.

5. Three to a Flush with Two Cards 10 or Higher and a Straight Possibility

It is not enough to have the flush chance, for there are two additional suited cards that must be matched up. We must also have the value of the two high cards, which can pair, and the possibility of the straight. The combination of all the above factors make this hand a profitable one to let the bet ride. An example of this hand is Q J 9 of clubs, or K J 9 of hearts.

6. Three to a Flush with J 9 8, 10 9 7 or 10 8 7

Unlike the above grouping, which can be played with a two gap straight possibility, these three hands have only one high card and are thus more marginal as a playable combination. They need the greater straight possibilities of the one gap hand (compared to the two gap straight in category 5) to make letting the bet ride a profitable play. These hands can also be thought of as a three card flush with one high card and one gap.

7. 10 J Q or J Q K

These hands, the most marginal of the seven categories, but still profitable enough to let the bet ride, provide two good possibilities for payoffs. First, any of the three cards, if paired, gives us a payoff with the added outside chance of trips on the fifth card; and second, both hands are open-ended straight possibilities that can fill into a winner paying 5-1.

Hands that We Won't Play

Similar hands to the seventh group of hands above that we won't play are A K Q, which is only a one-way, and therefore more difficult straight possibility to fill, and J 10 9, which has only two high cards that can pair into a payoff. On these marginal hands, we just don't have enough juice to justify the bet in circle 1, and the best percentage play is to take the bet down.

Other specific hands that should not be played are low pairs, that is, pairs less than 10's. For example, on the hand 7 7 Q, we should take down our bet. While you'll sometimes catch the third 7 or another Q, the times that you don't will more than overshadow the times you do, with a net long term result of a losing wager. That's exactly what we're trying to avoid.

And there you have it. Unless you have one of the hands in the seven categories listed in the above section, you should remove your bet from the first circle. While there are always winning possibilities with any three starting cards, the cost of playing low percentage hands is too costly to justify letting the bet ride.

Where you have a chance to remove a bet with inferior cards, you should always do so. That's the smart way to play.

Let's now move on to the strategy for the next round.

FOURTH CARD BETTING STRATEGY

After the dealer exposes one of the two community downcards, each player knows four of the five cards that will make up his or her final hand. We're faced with our final strategy decision: Should we let our bet ride, or should we reclaim it back into our bankroll?

As with the third card betting strategy, we'll play hands that give us a positive expectation of winning, and take down our bet in the second circle when our expectation of winning is negative. In the obvious cases where we already have a winning combination, the clear-cut play of course, is to let the bet ride. However, in many cases, we won't be quite as thrilled with our prospects, and would like nothing better than to take down our bet with our lousy cards.

Below, we'll look at the full strategy for letting bets ride or taking them down on circle 2.

Hands that We Will Play

We'll let our bet ride with the following four card hands.

1. Four of a Kind

This is an obvious winning hand paying 50-1. Let 'em ride!

2. Three or a Kind

This is also an obvious winner, paying 3-1 on all betting circles. Let 'em ride!

3. Two Pair - A clear-cut play

We already have a guaranteed 2-1 payoff with possibilities of improving to a full house for an 11-1 yield.

4. Pair of 10's or Higher Pair

We've already got a winner paying 1-1 and can improve to a two pair or three of a kind hand with a good draw on the final card.

5. Four to a Royal Flush

One more card, and we're there with a big pay-off. There are also the possibilities of making a flush or straight, and an excellent chance of catching a high paying pair since any of our four high cards, if matched, becomes a winner.

6. *Four to a Straight Flush*

This is not as strong as a four to a royal flush, but it is still holds excellent possibilities.

7. *Four to a Flush*

The payoff of 8-1 should the flush be drawn is greater than the odds of filling the flush, and is therefore an excellent bet. Of the 48 unseen cards in the deck, nine of them will make the flush, and 39 will not, odds of 4.33-1. Being paid 8-1 on odds of about 4.33-1 is always a great bet in my book.

8. *Four to an Open-Ended Straight*

When there are no high cards held, this bet is a wash. Of the 48 unseen cards, eight of them will make the straight, and 40 will not, odds of 5-1. Since the payoff is exactly 5-1, we have an even chance - there is no theoretical loss or gain on the play. We could choose to let our bet ride, or take it down.

If there is at least one high card as part of the open-ended straight, we now gain the advantage on the four card open ended straight draw, for the last community card may pair with our high card for a winner.

9. *Four to a High Straight*

The hands 10-J-Q-A, 10-Q-K-A, 10-J-K-A, and J-Q-K-A, have two things in common; the ability to match any of the four high cards into a paying winner, and the possibilities of filling to an inside straight. Neither factor by itself is enough to make the third bet, but together, due to the sensitivity of the single deck game, form enough strength to let the third bet ride, though marginally.

Hands that We Won't Play

We don't let our bet ride on circle 2 when holding a one way or inside straight, such as J 10 9 7, for the chances of making these one way straights climb to 11-1. Being paid at only 5-1 if the straight is made is not a good percentage bet. The one exception is the four card high straight, such as A K Q J, which combines pairing possibilities for all four cards. Small pairs, those 9's or under, are not worth chasing anymore. Our winning expectation is negative and since these hands promise no payoff as a 10's or better does, the best play in the long run is to take down the bet in circle 2.

Lacking any of the nine combinations listed above, in other words, holding hands of various degrees of junk, gives us a negative expectation on this fourth card and the strategy is clear - take down the bet and have it returned to your bankroll.

ADVANCED FINE PLAY STRATEGY - FOURTH CARD

Though you're not supposed to see the cards of your fellow players at the table, if you do, the extra information can be put to good use. Knowledge of cards that won't be put into play, either to help or hurt your hand or the dealer's, can be quite useful in determining the best way to play marginal hands and help you adjust your strategies for that extra edge.

In particular, the types of cards that would be useful to know in determining strategy changes are for those hands where folding the last bet could be affected by the cards you now know to be out of play. If you're looking to make an open-ended straight, and you see that three of your straight cards are held by other players at the table, this lets you know that your chances of hitting that straight are diminished. By the same token, if there are a bunch of Aces and Kings in play, then the chances of a dealer holding the minimum AK hand has diminished as well.

On the other hand, when you already have a good hand, such as a high pair, two pair, three or even four of a kind, it really doesn't affect your strategy whatever shows, because you already have a winning situation. No matter what cards you see in play, you'll still make the third bet. Also, consecutive or one gap straight flushes are so strong that losing some cards won't affect the proper play of letting the third bet ride.

Let's now look at several situations to see what types of strategy changes we'll make. In all the following discussions, the use of the term high card refers to any card 10, J, Q, K, or Ace, cards which when paired, will give you a payout. We'll assume that each player's hand that you see reveals three cards, that two players hands will reveal six cards, and three players hands, nine cards.

The fine point fourth card strategy presented here is only possible because Let it Ride is played as a single deck game. The removal of any card from play has an impact on the chances of receiving another like card, because there are only 52 cards total in the deck.

For example, if you need a queen to fill an inside straight, and see three queens in other players hands around the table, that gives you only one possibility of getting a queen to fill your straight. If, besides your cards, you have seen six other cards for a total of 10 known cards, it means that of the 42 unknown cards, there is only one queen to be had, odds of 1 in 42 – very long odds.

Contrasting this with a six deck game, which currently is not used in Let it Ride, the effect, though felt, is not as severe. Of the 312 cards, 10 are known, 302 are not. Six decks starts with 24 queens. With three queens out, there are still 21 remaining, odds of about 1 in 14, a significant difference from the single deck situation. In fact, the chances of a queen being turned over in the six deck game with three queens removed for this particular situation, are almost three times greater than that of the single deck game as we've seen in the above example.

This sensitivity to particular card removal in single deck Let it Ride, affects multiple situations, and may cause strategy changes on hands that are near marginal without knowledge of additional cards.

Note that the fine points presented in this section are not crucial knowledge for the regular player and should only be digested if you want that little extra edge.

CONSECUTIVE STRAIGHTS
Hand One - Low Four Card Straight
    With no high cards, 10, J, Q, K, or Ace, as part of the straight, this hand is a marginal call situation.

See one neighbor's hand

Don't make the third bet if you see any straight card you need.

See two or three neighbor's hands

Don't make the third bet if you see two or more straight cards you need.

Hand Two - 7, 8, 9, 10

The one high card straight hand, 7, 8, 9, 10, is a little stronger than the hand above, owing to the added possibilities of pairing the 10.

See one neighbor's hand

Don't make the third bet if you see a combination of two or more 6's or J's, cards that you need to fill the straight. Removal of these cards is enough to make your hand's prospects negative. Even if you see three 10's removed, all cards which hurt your chances of pairing for a payout, you still have a good enough percentage to make the third bet.

This is the same thinking as if you started with a 3, 4, 5, 6 type hand anyway, a low straight without any possibility of pairing high. While the removal of these three 10's, hurt your chances at pairing high, on the positive side, they do help your chances of filling the straight.

See two neighbor's hands

You still take down the bet if you see two or more straight cards you need.

See three neighbor's hands

Play if two straight cards are out, even if one or two 10's show, but take down the bet if a third card needed for the straight is seen.

Hand Three - 8, 9, 10, J

This hand is progressively a little stronger again, having two high cards that can pair into winners along with the open-ended straight.

See one neighbor's hand

This hand will be played for the last bet if a combination of two 7's and Q's are out, however, if a third Q or 7 is viewed, take down the last bet. Even if three 10's or J's are in the one hand you see, the straight remains strong enough to let the bet ride.

See two neighbor's hands

Play the same strategy as above.

See three neighbor's hands

The bet gets taken down only if four 7's and Q's are seen among the fellow players. If just three are viewed, the third bet should stay intact on the table–let it ride.

NON-CONSECUTIVE STRAIGHTS
Hand Four - 10, J, Q, A - 10, Q, K, A - 10, J, K, A - J, Q, K, A

The four card inside straight gives you four cards to pair for a 1-1 payoff, along with the possibilities of filling inside for a 5-1 payoff. Being an inside straight makes this hand marginally good to play only with everything going right. However, if additional information informs us otherwise, our strategy will get adjusted.

See one neighbor's hand

Take down the third bet if any straight card gets seen. The loss of this added card that can pay 5-1 makes the overall play on the negative side of marginal, and the bet should not ride. Also, take down the bet if two high cards that can pair are viewed.

See two neighbor's hands

Take down the bet if any straight card or three high pairing cards are viewed.

See three neighbor's hands

Two straight cards being viewed is enough to take down the bet. The bet rides even if a whole bunch of high pairing cards are viewed. Their removal, though not optimal, helps the chances of the straight filling, and there are still plenty of high cards to pair for a payoff.

Hand Five - 8, 10, J, Q

This four card inside straight has three high cards (one less than the above hand) and normally wouldn't get played. However, under the right circumstances, it would be worth a play on the third bet.

See one neighbor's hand

As usual, take down the bet, regardless of what cards you see.

See two neighbor's hands

Let the third bet ride only if no detrimental cards are seen. That is, if you see any 9, 10, J, or Q in play, the 9 being the straight card, the others being high pairing cards, then the bet is taken down.

See three neighbor's hands

With any straight card appearing in any player's hand, or two or more high pairing cards in play, the usual play is made–the bet is taken down. Let the bet ride though, if one high pairing card is seen.

VII. LET IT RIDE VIDEO VERSION

The video version of Let it Ride is played similarly to the table game, and was introduced to casinos after the table game began establishing itself in the casinos. The original video versions were introduced on Bally machine platforms but didn't fare as well as Shuffle Master had hoped.

In this section, we'll talk about the original machines and their difficulties, the new generations coming out, and some strategies to follow when playing Let it Ride on the video versions.

THE FIRST GENERATION MACHINES

The problem with the first generation Let it Ride video games was not in the game itself, but in the players' unfamiliarity with it. The machines were designed to give players a good shot at winning, but the actual results under real conditions had the opposite effect. There was even one video version on the market that put the player at only 1/2 percent disadvantage with proper play, very low by casino standards, but the average player was still taking a terrible beating.

It turned out that too many players were uninformed or confused about the proper play of the game and the correct strategies to follow, and as a result, were letting their second and third bets ride way too often–contrary to the correct playing strategy. As we learned earlier, it is far too costly to let the second and third bets ride, unless the situation favors the player. These poor percentage bets caused players to lose money so fast that they soon tired of the game and moved on elsewhere where luck smiled on them more favorably.

Profit margins were high in these machines, but for the players taste, too high. With so many players faring poorly, the Let it Ride video game became less popular than was hoped. Overall profits dropped, and that's not good for business. Shuffle Master was looking for high volume play, and instead ended up disappointed.

Shuffle Master's mixed success with the early video versions of Let it Ride led to a re-thinking of their approach. Below, we'll show a few paytables that were offered on these first machines.

Basic Paytables

The first paytable shown has a frequency of wins for the player at over 30%, but the overall payouts are not as good as the one shown on the next page.

LET IT RIDE $1 BASIC PAYTABLE
Video Machine - A

Royal Flush	$1,000
Straight Flush	$100
Four of a Kind	$50
Full House	$8
Flush	$6
Straight	$5
Three of a Kind	$4
Two Pairs	$3
Jacks or Better	$2
8's, 9's, or 10's	$1

Here is another version of a paytable with a frequency of wins for the player at over 30%. Winning hands pay more here than the paytable shown on the previous page.

LET IT RIDE $1 BASIC PAYTABLE
Video Machine - B

Royal Flush	$1,000
Straight Flush	$100
Four of a Kind	$50
Full House	$9
Flush	$7
Straight	$6
Three of a Kind	$4
Two Pairs	$3
Jacks or Better	$2
8's, 9's, or 10's	$1

This paytable is a bit more liberal than the previous one, with the full house getting $10 (instead of $9 and $8 on the previous ones), as well as better payoffs on the flush and straight hands.

LET IT RIDE $1 BASIC PAYTABLE
Video Machine - C

Royal Flush	$1,000
Straight Flush	$100
Four of a Kind	$50
Full House	$10
Flush	$8
Straight	$7
Three of a Kind	$4
Two Pairs	$3
Jacks or Better	$2
8's, 9's, or 10's	$1

Bonus Paytables

The following Bonus Paytable shows a typical payout for the $1 bonus bet. As we mentioned earlier, these models are being phased out and the new machines, as currently planned, will probably not include the bonus wager.

LET IT RIDE $1 BONUS PAYOUT Video Bonus Machine - A	
Royal Flush	$20,000
Straight Flush	$2,000
Four of a Kind	$200
Full House	$75
Flush	$50
Straight	$25
Three of a Kind	$8
Two Pairs	$4
Jacks or Better	$1
8's, 9's, or 10's	No Payout

Here is another version of the paytable which was quite unfavorable for the player. This particular schedule shows the full payout including the $1 bet, thus, the two pair hand is really giving the player only a 1-1 payoff.

Notice the much bigger payouts on the hands rarely hit, four of a kind and above, and the smaller payouts on hands hit more frequently. This schedule also requires a two pair or better hand to win.

LET IT RIDE $1 BONUS PAYOUT
Video Bonus Machine - B

Royal Flush	$100,000
Straight Flush	$5,000
Four of a Kind	$500
Full House	$100
Flush	$50
Straight	$20
Three of a Kind	$5
Two Pairs	$2
Jacks or Better	No Payout
8's, 9's, or 10's	No Payout

THE NEW MODELS

In the new 1998-1999 versions of the Let it Ride video machines, which will be deliverd on the IGT video slots platform, Shuffle Master has made some changes that they hope will spur interest in their revamped versions. As we go to press, some of their plans with the new machines are as yet unclear and await testing in the casinos, but we've managed to obtain some preliminary plans about the nature of the new configurations.

Two important changes will probably be incorporated into the new designs.

First of all, to simplify the game and give regular players a good return, the biggest change will be to eliminate the $1 bonus bet. The new Let it Ride video games will feature only the basic paytable.

The second important change will be to reduce the maximum allowed bet from five units to three units on each of the betting circles. Thus, a player would insert nine coins maximum to play the video machine, three coins on each of the betting circles available.

So overall, where the old machines took a total of 16 coins, five on each betting circle and the bonus bet, the new ones hit the player for only nine coins total. That's a substantial amount less for players to put at risk, and should reduce overall losses for the players.

Less losses means more winners, which for players, translates to more play for the buck.

At the time of this writing, Shuffle Master had not yet decided on the paytables they would offer the players, but my sources there indicated that they were going to offer players a reasonable shake to induce play. Their biggest challenge, they said, was to reduce the risk of exposure for players that didn't know how to play, so that they could keep these players interested.

The company will go through a testing period and offer various paytables in different venues to see which ones generate the most interest. While they have offered some excellent payoff schedules, at the same time, there have been some largely unfavorable ones as well, so we'll have to see what holds in the marketplace.

WINNING STRATEGIES

The strategies on the new machines will be identical to the table games if the same winning hands are required for a payoff. However, if that is not the case, you will need to adjust your strategies according to the paytable itself.

For example, on some of the machines, a minimum hand of eights or better might qualify for a payoff. If this is the actual payoff on the machine you're playing, you would have to adjust your thinking to incorporate eights and nines as high cards. These cards, of course, would be in addition to the tens or better. If nines or sevens are used, you'll need to adjust accordingly as well.

Below, we'll just highlight a few basic ideas to keep in mind for playing strategy.

Third Card Betting Strategy

As in the table version, we automatically let the bets ride for any hands that offer an automatic payout. There is nothing to lose in these situations. At a minimum, there is a paying winner, and if there is a lucky draw, a bigger winner.

We'll also play strong hands that don't yet have a guaranteed payoff but which have a positive winning expectation. Similarly, with poor cards, we always want to use the unique feature of the game that allows us to remove our bet from the table

If you have pairs less than 8's, one way straights, and any weak hands, you should remove your bet from the first circle. The cost of playing low percentage hands is too costly to justify letting the bet ride.

Fourth Card Betting Strategy

When we already have a winning hand, the obvious strategy is to let the bet ride. We'll also let our bets ride with very good straight, flush, straight flush, and royal flush possibilities.

By the same token, bets should be taken down when the cards held have no winners or little future of winning. Actually, we'll only let the bet ride when our hand gives us an outright advantage.

With none of the solid combinations that are automatic winners or show great promise, take down the last bet. Do not be tempted to play weak hands in the hopes that your weak four card hand can improve to a winner on a lucky draw. That will happen sometimes, but the problem is that you'll lose money in the long run trying to squeeze a few winners out of poor starting cards.

VIII. HOUSE PERCENTAGES

HOUSE PERCENTAGE OVERVIEW

The best percentage that can be achieved at the Let it Ride table games is about 3.5% against the player for the basic bets. This is assuming that the player uses the optimal basic strategy we present here and that the $1 bet is not made on the tournament or bonus bet spots.

Less than optimal play at the table can cost the player multiple percentage points, the severity of which depends on the number of mistakes or poor decisions made. The more of an edge the player gives the house, on average, the more money that player will lose when he or she plays.

For example, a player who doesn't let his bets ride on automatic winning hands or who lets his bets ride on terrible starting cards, will increase the house edge precipitously.

Players who make bets on the optional $1 tournament or bonus spot are giving the casino a much larger edge, an edge that varies depending upon the payouts for the particular casino played in.

Making poor percentage bets will raise the overall house edge higher than the 3.5% stated here. The smaller the average bet, the higher that house percentage would be. For example, a poor percentage $1 bet has a greater overall negative effect on an average $5 bettor than an average $25 bettor.

In the video versions of Let it Ride, the player may find better chances of winning due to a more aggressive payout schedule. This was the case with some early machines, but there was also versions that put the player at a less than desirable disadvantage. Keep in mind that the frequency of play is so much greater on a video machine than a table game, that every percentage point disadvantage the player faces at a Let it Ride video machine is magnified and will show up as bigger losses.

For example, at a table game, a player may get dealt about 50-60 hands per hour, more if there is just one player gambling there. But at a machine, a super fast player can get in as many as 600 plays per hour, while an average player can do perhaps 300-500 plays.

While the Shuffle Master orgainization is still

experimenting with the exact form of machine they will be offering customers, a simple check of the payout schedule may give you a good idea as to whether you're getting a better game or not.

ODD OF DRAWING HANDS

Following is a table showing the odds of getting dealt winning hands in Let it Ride. These are the same odds as those in regular draw poker (first five cards dealt) and Caribbean Stud Poker.

Odds of Drawing Winning Hands	
Royal Flush	649,739 -1
Straight Flush	72,192 -1
Four of a Kind	4,165 -1
Full House	693 -1
Flush	508 -1
Straight	254 -1
Three of a Kind	46 -1
Two Pair	20 -1
One Pair	1.37 -1

MORE PERCENTAGES OF PLAY

Our general strategy in Let it Ride resembles that of blackjack's basic strategy in that we try to minimize losses when we're dealt poor cards, and maximize gains when our cards are strong. Thus, while many two card totals in blackjack will be played from a perspective of losing the least amount of money, strong hands, when possible, will be doubled down to take advantage of the strong situation by getting more money on the bets.

Similarly, in Let it Ride, most starting hands have losing expectations for the player. In fact, 85 out of 100 times (actually 84.5%), the correct playing strategy dictates that both the first and second bets would be removed, and that only the third bet, the one that cannot be removed, be played. It is the other 15% of the time, where the player's hand is in an advantageous situation, that more money is wagered in the form of letting the second or third bets ride.

Again, just like in blackjack, we take advantage of our profitable situation by making sure money is bet on our hand. It is on these occasions, particularly when all three bets are riding, where the larger losses of the 85% of the hands that are dealt to a losing expectation are made up by betting more in a winning situation. Those second and third bets are where we make up lost ground. Like any good gambling strategy, the general rule is: minimize losses and maximize gains.

Using the proper playing strategy, a total of two bets will stay in action about 8.5% of the time, and the full three bets, 7.0% of the time.

When all three situations are added up, the wagers with one bet, the wagers with two bets and the wagers with three bets, the house edge will emerge at 3.5% at the table version of Let it Ride if our playing strategy is followed.

Frequency of Wins

To get a winning payout of any kind will occur about one hand in four, 23.88% at the time, at either of the two basic Let it Ride paytables. On the Bonus paytables, the frequency of winning will range up to 23.88% if the same number of payoffs are given, and less, of course, when there are fewer payoffs to be had.

The video version of Let it Ride that offers payouts on eights or better, gives the player a frequency at winning of about three times in ten, or 30.38% to be exact. If the machines offer payouts for hands of tens or better, then these video units, of course, would have the same 23.88% frequency of winning as the table game.

STRATEGY OVERVIEW

The 3.5% house edge in the Let it Ride basic table game on the three bet circles is higher than the overall 2.56% of Caribbean Stud Poker when the call and ante bets are combined, and other table games such as blackjack, baccarat and craps, when those games are played properly. It is also higher than single zero roulette, which is starting to become more prevalent in U.S. casinos.

The big draw for the original versions of Let it Ride was the $1 tournament bet and the hope of hitting a monster hand. However, this wager is much worse than the 3.5% edge of the basic game, and the new Bonus game, with that same $1 bet depending upon the payout schedule offered, can be poor as well.

For my taste, I don't like making high percentage negative bets, and if I do, I might be more apt to go for the multi-millions of the lottery with that same $1 bet. But then again, as opposed to the lottery, Let it Ride lets players participate in the action, make decisions that effect the outcome of the game, and of course, can be part of the casino experience.

It is my recommendation that players who want the best odds possible at Let it Ride stay away from the $1 tournament or bonus bets due to the typical poor odds of these wagers, but of course, other considerations must be taken in as well.

The overall attraction of the extra bonus bet is that it gives players a chance to win large sums of money with just a $1 wager. Again, making a comparison with the lottery, while these bets may not have the glamour of the million dollar jackpot offered by lottery games, they do offer odds that are worlds better than the lottery hustles.

And with much better chances of winning something good for just a little money, the Let it Ride bonus bet has become popular among players. And since fun is what gambling is supposed to be about, if you don't mind the steeper odds, at least you have a much better shot at winning something here than throwing a buck away on the numbers game.

IX. WINNING REMINDER

For players to give themselves the best chances of winning at Let it Ride, they'll need to study the third and fourth card playing strategies, keeping only the bets which give them a positive expectation of winning, and taking down those bets where the hand doesn't justify the extra money wagered. It is always best to play the optimal strategy so that the casino edge is brought down to the bare edge possible.

Let it Ride, like all gambling pursuits, is subject to the ups and downs of winning and losing streaks. Players must make sure to keep their losing streaks to reasonable and acceptable levels, and when winning, to walk away with the casino's money.

SECTION IV

MONEY MANAGEMENT

INTRODUCTION

To be a winner at Caribbean Stud Poker and Let it Ride, a player must not only gamble intelligently, but must also make proper use of one's bankroll and keep his or her emotions under control.

The tendency to ride a winning streak too hard in the hope of a big killing or to bet wildly during a losing streak attempting a quick comeback, have spelled doom to many a session which otherwise may have been a good win. Wins can turn into losses, and moderate losses can turn into a nightmare.

There is perhaps no strategy more important than a smart money management strategy. Winning and losing streaks are a very real part of gambling. It is how one deals with the inherent ups and downs at the tables that determines just how well a gambler will fare at the tables. In this chapter, we're going to present the sage advice every gambler should and must take to heart, for money management is a vital part of the winning formula. Everything I say here is common sense, yet is the downfall of a majority of gamblers, who nonetheless, follow the beat of some temporary madness, and manage to squander away good winnings or let themselve be taken to the cleaners.

You may be playing at an advantage or disadvantage to the house in a particular game, or at a particular time but just because you're playing at an advantage doesn't mean you'll win in the short run, and conversely, just because you're playing at a disadvantage doesn't mean you'll lose. Anything can happen in the short run.

And that's why money management is so important. When you're winning, you have to stretch those winnings to the maximum safe level and make sure you finish a winner. And when things go the other direction, you must restrict losses to affordable amounts and protect yourself from ever really getting hurt at the tables.

If you follow the advice in this section, you'll be playing accoridng to the same principles as professional gamblers, and making the best use of your monetary resources. You'll always keep losses under control—and control is always a key concept in gambling—while winning sessions always end up as winning sessions.

You'll be on your way to successful gambling and when your luck falls right, you'll be a winner!

THE RISKS OF OVERBETTING

Astute gamblers have one thing in common—they know how to manage their money. Superior playing skills alone does not make one a winning player. The concept here is self control, the ability of a player to keep the game in check and never to lose sight of the winning strategies.

We'll show a simple example of how overbetting can quickly change a big winning session into a disaster. Let's say a bettor starts out with a bankroll of $250, has been betting $5-$20 a shot and after two hours of strong play has ridden a surge of luck to $225 in winnings. Now he has $475 in front of him.

Getting greedy and caught up in the excitement of the game, the gambler now really wants to put the squeeze on and fast, so he goes against his pre-planned strategy, if he even has one, and now goes for $50 -$100 a bet. With a little luck and a few big wins in a row, he's on easy street.

However, after three straight losses at $100 a pop, he gets frantic, and goes for one more play at $175, pushing all his money on the wager. Make or break. Another loss.

Suddenly, a careful strategy that netted $225 got changed into "if I can get lucky on this play, please" strategy, and the player is out $250!

Madness. Here was an example of a winning player losing control, betting over his head, and taking what by all rights was a tremendous winning session and finishing four bets later out all his bankroll! And this was an example using hundreds of dollars. Many gamblers play at this same scenario with thousands of dollars, and some get beaten up with bad decisions to the tune of tens of thousands of dollars.

And what if the sequence went a little differently, and more of those big bets were won rather than lost, so that instead the player sat with $500 in winnings. We all know that type of player, and know that he wouldn't have left until the game broke him. Bets would have been raised again and then he would have been bankrupted. Or the next session would have done the job.

To win, you must want to win, and want to win bad enough that you won't give that money back to the casino.

MONEY MANAGEMENT CONCEPTS

I'm going to present a very important concept that, if followed, will put a lot money money in your pocket.

KEY MONEY MANAGEMENT #1

Once you have won money from a casino, that money is yours, and not the casino's.

If you have $150 in winnings in front of you, you are not playing with the casino's money. It is your money now! If you think of your winnings as the casino's money, you won't feel bad giving it back. That's a dangerous attitude. Think of the money as yours now, and you won't be wanting to hand it back. And now maybe you'll walk away from the table with those winnings.

Let's move on *the* most important concept in money management.

KEY MONEY MANAGEMENT #2

Never gamble with money that you cannot afford to lose, either financially, or emotionally.

Do not gamble with needed funds no matter how "sure" the bet seems. The possibilities of taking a loss are real, and if that loss will hurt, you're playing with fire. Don't be coming into town, as they say, in a $20,000 Cadillac and leaving in a $100,000 Greyhound.

Gambling with needed funds is a foolish gamble, for gambling involves chance, and the short term possibilities of taking a loss are real, no matter how easy the game may appear, or how well the odds are stacked in your favor. Unexpected things happen in gambling, that's what makes it so interesting. But if you never play over your head, you'll never suffer.

Gambling is a form of entertainment and if you can't afford the possibility of losing - don't gamble at the stakes you were considering. Either play at lower levels or don't gamble at all. If the larger wagers of your gambling game make your adrenaline rush too hard, you're over your head and need to find a game with lower limits.

But don't overlook the emotional side as well. If the playing of the game becomes a cause of undue anxiety, for whatever the reason, than it ceases to be a form of entertainment and you need a break. Take some time away from the game, be it a coffee break or a month's rest.

Playing under anxiety not only ruins the fun of the game but also adversely affects play and can influence you to make decisions contrary to what smart strategy dictates.

Let's make clear one final very important concept in money management, a concept which you must always keep in mind when gambling.

KEY MONEY MANAGEMENT #3

Your goal in gambling is not just to win, but to get satisfaction out of the game. Keep that in mind and you can never go wrong.

THE NATURE OF THE GAMBLE

In any gambling pursuit where luck plays a role, fluctuations in ones fortunes are common. It is the ability of the player to successfully deal with the ups and downs inherent in the gamble, that separate the smart gamblers from the losers.

You can't always win - even when the odds favor you - and you won't always lose, even when the odds are against you. In the short run, anything can happen and usually does. But over the long run, luck evens itself out, and it is skill, in the bets one makes and how one plays the game, that will determine if a player is a winner or a loser.

The smart player bides his time, is patient, keeps the game under control and as a result can win when the odds are in his favor.

PROPER BANKROLLING

Betting too high for one's bankroll leaves a player vulnerable in two ways. First, a normal downward trend can wipe out a limited money supply and put the player out of commission. Second, and equally important, the bettor may feel pressured by the shortage of capital and play less optimally than smart play dictates.

I don't know how often I have seen players avoid the correct double down in blackjack because they were pressured by a shortage of capitol, or a Let it Ride player going for extra bets they shouldn't be making in the hopes of a bigger win, or even in Caribbean Stud, where a player incessantly dumped $1 into the progressive in the hopes of getting lucky enough to turn a run of bad luck into a sudden win.

These are all bad signs, indications of a player being pressured by capitol to make bets that otherwise wouldn't be made. That's not smart gambling, though it's what the casinos love to see.

If the amount staked on a bet is above your head, you're playing in the wrong game. Play in a lower limit game–at levels of betting you feel comfortable with.

KNOW WHEN TO QUIT

What often separates the winners from the losers is that the winners, when winning, leave the table a winner, and when losing, restrict their losses to affordable amounts. Smart gamblers never allow themselves to get destroyed at the table.

Minimizing losses is the key. You can't always win. If you're losing, keep the losses affordable–take a break. You only want to play with a clear head.

MINIMIZING LOSSES

The key concept in minimizing losses during a bad gambling run is to set up a stop-loss limit. Before sitting at the table and making your bets, you must decide on the amount of money you'll put at stake, and should luck turn against you, restrict your losses to that amount only.

Do not go against this rule and you can never take a big beating. If things go poorly at first, take a break - simple as that. There will always be losing streaks; it's how you handle them that counts.

When you're winning big, put a good chunk of these winnings in a "don't touch" pile, and play with the rest. You never want to hand all your winnings back to the casino. Should a losing streak occur, you're out of there - a winner!!!

PROTECTING YOUR WINS

Once you've accumulated a sizable win at the tables, the most important thing is to walk away a winner. There is no worse feeling than skulking away from a table after having lost all your wins back.

The general guidelines I recommend is to put away half to two thirds of your winnings into a "protected" area that you won't touch under any circumstances. That money is bankable, for you won't play it. Keep playing with the rest of the winnings, putting more aside as the wins accumulate. Once the streak stops and the tides of fortune go against you, you'll leave the table a guaranteed winner for you've played it smart!

For example, let's say you're up 20 units. (A unit is the bet size you're using as a standard and could be $1, $5, $10, $25, $100, $500 or whatever value you want to assign.) Let's say your unit size is $5, so you're up $100. Put aside $50 (10 units) of your winnings into the protected zone and play the other $50 (10 units).

Set no limits on a winning streak. When you've got a hot hand, ride it for all its worth.

INCREASING BETS WHEN WINNING

If you want to risk more to win more, go for it - but in moderation. Increase your bets gradually when winning, never getting overzealous as in the earlier example.

For example, if your bet size is a flat $10 in a game, and winnings are rapidly accumulating, jump up to $15, and if all goes well, to $20. This way if you keep winning, the wins get larger. If however, a sudden losing streak ensues, no problem, for you have protected yourself.

This constant attention to squirreling away chips when winning into protected piles will make it impossible for casinos to get any of your money back when you've got the hot hand. As long as the winnings are coming in, good, you keep on betting. Once there is a downturn, which will come soon enough, you're gone, with plenty of the casinos money lining your pockets.

SECTION V

LAST THOUGHTS

IN CONCLUSION

We've covered a lot of ground in this book, looking at the rules and strategies for Let it Ride and Caribbean Stud Poker, the thinking behind some of the plays you should make, and the key elements of Money Management. It is now up to you as a player, to heed the advice in this book, and when gambling, to try to be a tough player, one who's serious about walking away from the tables as a winner.

Play smart and never give the casino any edge you can keep on your side of the equation. As I've tried to stress throughout this book, you want to give yourself every opportunity to emerge a winner. That means you must make the best bets,and stay focused on winning. And of course, you must play intelligently, according to the sound money management principles we covered earlier. That's the best way to give yourself every opportunity to walk from the tables with the casinos money in your pocket.

Gambling involves real money being put at stake, so before playing for real, it is best to prepare yourself for the casinos. My advice is to first reread the strategies presented here for the games you'll be playing. Go over them carefully until you are sure you understand them and can use them comfortably.

Second, you should practice them at home until the proper plays that should be made become second nature to your game. The most effective way for most players to practice is by dealing out hands as they would in a casino. The repetition achieved by dealing out hands at home is a valuable tool to learning. If hands get dealt that leave you unsure as to the proper strategy, then you need more practice. However, once you've got all the strategies down cold, you're ready to play and give the game your best shot.

Remember that both Let it Ride and Caribbean Stud Poker are negative expectation games–the house has the edge and your expectaction is to lose in the long run. These are not games that can be approached on a professional level. No matter how perfectly you follow the strategies we present, you can't change the nature of the fact that the house has a built-in edge. But by playing the best game you can, you cut down the house edge to the lowest possible amount, and leave the window open to turn a run of luck into winnings.

Remember winning is the goal. Good skill!!

SAITEK'S GREAT HANDHELD CASINO GAMES!

The World Leader in Intelligent Electronic games

We're stocking these great handheld computer games again! These **exciting palm-sized** games fit into your pockets and can be taken anywhere - they're great travel items! **Easy-to-use**, you'll be playng in just a few seconds. Large LCD screens and superb sound effects bring the excitement and challenge of Las Vegas casino play to you. **High end** line has advance game functions, and streamline designs with lids. Includes automatic five minute powerdown.

PRO BLACKJACK - $39.95

Have fun and learn to win at the same time with this great blackjack computer. Has all the features: choose from 1- 6 deck games, and from 1-3 players at the table. Follows Las Vegas rules and allows $10 to $1,000 bets - hey big spender! Built-in hint key gives advice on all situations and even introduces you to card counting! Has superb casino sounds.

CRAPS PROFESSOR - $79.95

Brand New! The ultimate in craps simulations, this very handsome unit is an electronic trainer *and* game. Follows Las Vegas rules, make all the bets - pass, don't pass, come, don't come, free odds, buy, lay, place and proposition wagers! use electronic dice or roll your own (dice provided). Great casino sounds enhance experience. Comes with comprehensive book, hint cards, and winning strategy cards. Lots of fun!

PRO ROULETTE - $39.95

Beautiful unit has full layout and wheel with all the legal bets plus up to 12 wagers allowing from 1-199 bets! Make any number bet you want, game plays according to the real rules. Even better, up to three can play. Auto power off remembers game; turn on again another time and continue playing. Place your bets, and spin the wheel!!

BUY ONE OR BUY ALL! GREAT GIFTS!

Yes! I'm ready to play! Buy one or buy all! Enclosed is a check or money order for each game desired (plus postage and handling), made out to:

Cardoza Publishing, P.O. Box 1500, Cooper Station, New York, NY 10276

Call Toll-Free in U.S. & Canada, 1-800-577-WINS

Fax Orders (718)743-8284 - E-Mail Orders: CardozaPub@aol.com

Include $5.00 shipping first game ordered, $2.00 each additional one for U.S; double for Can/Mex; HI/AK and other countries 4x (four times). Outside U.S., money order payable in U.S. dollars on U.S. bank only.

ITEM DESIRED _____ _____ _____

NAME _____

ADDRESS _____

CITY _____ STATE _____ ZIP _____

Order Today! 30 Day Money Back Guarantee!   Carib/Ride

Baccarat Master Card Counter
New Winning Strategy!

For the **first time**, Gambling Research Institute releases the **latest winning techniques** at baccarat. This **exciting** strategy, played by big money players in Monte Carlo and other exclusive locations, is based on principles that have made insiders and pros **hundreds of thousands of dollars** counting cards at blackjack - card counting!

NEW WINNING APPROACH
This brand **new** strategy now applies card counting to baccarat to give you a **new winning approach,** and is designed so that any player, with just a **little effort**, can successfully take on the casinos at their own game - and win!

SIMPLE TO USE, EASY TO MASTER
You learn how to count cards for baccarat without the mental effort needed for blackjack! No need to memorize numbers - keep the count on the scorepad. Easy-to-use, play the strategy while enjoying the game!

LEARN WHEN TO BET BANKER, WHEN TO BET PLAYER
No longer will you make bets on hunches and guesses - use the GRI Baccarat Master Card Counter to determine when to bet Player and when to bet Banker. You learn the basic counts (running and true), deck favorability, when to increase bets and much more in this **winning strategy.**

LEARN TO WIN IN JUST ONE SITTING
That's right! After **just one sitting** you'll be able to successfully learn this powerhouse strategy and use it to your advantage at the baccarat table. Be the best baccarat player at the table - the one playing the odds to **win**! Baccarat can be beaten. The Master Card Counter shows you how!

To order send just $50 (plus postage and handling) by check or money order to:
Cardoza Publishing, P.O. Box 1500, Cooper Station, New York, NY 10276

THE CARDOZA CRAPS MASTER

Exclusive Offer! - Not Available Anywhere Else)
Three Big Strategies!

Here it is! **At last**, the **secrets** of the **Grande-Gold Power Sweep, Molliere's Monte Carlo Turnaround** and the **Montarde-D'Girard Double Reverse** - three big strategies - are made available and presented for the **first time anywhere!** These powerful strategies are designed for the serious craps player, one wishing to bring the best odds and strategies to hot tables, cold tables and choppy tables.

I. THE GRANDE-GOLD POWER SWEEP (HOT TABLE STRATEGY)

This **dynamic strategy** takes maximum advantage of hot tables and shows you how to amass small **fortunes quickly** when numbers are being thrown fast and furious. The Grande-Gold stresses aggressive betting on wagers the house has no edge on! This previously unreleased strategy will make you a powerhouse at a hot table.

2. MOLLIERE'S MONTE CARLO TURNAROUND (COLD TABLE STRATEGY)

For the player who likes betting against the dice, Molliere's Monte Carlo Turnaround shows how to turn a cold table into hot cash. Favored by an exclusive circle of professionals who will play nothing else, the uniqueness of this strongman strategy is that the vast majority of bets **give absolutely nothing away to the casino!**

3.MONTARDE-D'GIRARD DOUBLE REVERSE (CHOPPY TABLE STRATEGY)

This **new** strategy is the **latest development** and the **most exciting strategy** to be designed in recent years. **Learn how** to play the optimum strategies against the tables when the dice run hot and cold (a choppy table) with no apparent reason. **The Montarde-d'Girard Double Reverse** shows how you can **generate big profits** while less knowledgeable players are ground out by choppy dice. And, of course, the majority of our bets give nothing away to the casino!

BONUS!!!

Order now, and you'll receive **The Craps Master-Professional Money Management Formula** ($15 value) **absolutely free!** Necessary for serious players and **used by the pros**, the Craps Master Formula features the unique **stop-loss ladder.**

The Above Offer is Not Available Anywhere Else. You Must Order Here.

To order send ~~$75~~ $50 (plus postage and handling) by check or money order to:
Cardoza Publishing, P.O. Box 1500, Cooper Station, New York, NY 10276

AVERY CARDOZA'S CASINO 2000

The Complete Casino Experience & Professional Gambling Tutor
For IBM-Compatibles (Win 3.1/95/NT/98) - Requires CD-ROM, 486/66 or better

65 GAME VARIETIES! - LOADED WITH FEATURES! - UP TO 3 CAN PLAY!

A GREAT TIME AWAITS! Enter Avery Cardoza's incredible **multi-player** 3D casino where you're *really* **part of the action!** 65 great game varieties include 1, 2, 4, *and* 6 deck blackjack, double odds craps, 40 different slot machines including progressive, 17 video poker machines, including progressive, big table roulette, and keno with a 100,000 game memory. **It's all here!**

YOU HAVE COMPLETE INTERACTION! Choose any of 4 ways to roll the dice *and* how long to roll 'em in craps; play up to three hands in blackjack; go for a royal flush in video poker; pull for the slots jackpot; make over 150 roulette bets; bet keno anytime - game is always playing!

INTERACTIVE 3D DEALERS ALSO! Dealers shuffle, deal, call the games, and react to your every move. **1803** responses tied to **257** criteria makes for dealers so intelligent and realistic, you never know what they'll say or do!

EXPERT ON-LINE TUTOR! Don't know what to do? Use *Ask the Expert* to learn the best play for *every* situation in *every* game!; or use the *Coach* to alert on bad plays, or turn off to go solo!

FREE BONUS BOOK - $15 VALUE! Learn the rules of play and how to use **professional strategies** with your $15 Avery Cardoza strategy book - included **free!**

MORE PROFESSIONAL FEATURES! 577 statistical fields keep track of *every* vital stat: your percentage of correct plays, most profitable sessions, the number of full houses or straights, number of blackjacks, hours of play, peak win levels, hot and cold trends, biggest craps shoot or slots jackpot, average win per bet - and 500 more fields! Also displays all fields as graphs!

AVERY CARDOZA'S VIDEO POKER 2000

The Complete Video Poker Experience & Professional Gambling Tutor
For IBM-Compatibles (Win 3.1/95/NT/98)- Requires CD-ROM, 486/66 or better

36 GREAT MACHINES! - TWO FREE BONUS SLOTS ALSO!

• **THIRTY-SIX DIFFERENT VARIATIONS!** This is the real deal with Jacks or Better, Deuces Wild, and Joker Wild, Progressive Jackpots, Double Progressive Jackpots, Triple Progressive Jackpots, Bonus Quads, Bonus Royals, Double Up Games, Double Joker, Five Deck Poker, Tens or Better, Triple Play, Two Pairs or Better, Deuces and Joker Wild, Double Down Stud, Double or Nothing, Second Chance, and more!

• **SUPER FEATURES!** Features photorealistic art, winning payoff bells, statistical tracking for up to 20 players, liberal payouts, credit button, hold/discard, and even a cashout button with tumbling coins, put you right in the action ready to set the bells off! Let's play!!

• **ASK THE EXPERT FEATURE!** Based on Avery Cardoza's professional advice, this great feature lets you know the optimal play for any situation; simply click on the Ask the Expert button. Every combination of cards for every variety is covered – millions of possibilities in all!

• **TURN ON THE LEARNING MODE!** Go from beginner to pro. Based on the professional winning strategies used by Avery Cardoza, this feature chimes every time an incorrect play is made and gives you the chance to use the expert advice or play on with your own decision.

• **FREE BONUS BOOK! ($15.00 VALUE)!** Receive *Avery Cardoza's Video Poker 2000 Strategy guide* by gambling guru **Avery Cardoza**. This $15.00 strategy guide is included free!